JAPAN

JAPAN
The New Superstate

Nobutaka Ike
STANFORD UNIVERSITY

Trade distributor: Charles Scribner's Sons, New York

W. H. FREEMAN AND COMPANY
San Francisco

Library of Congress Cataloging in Publication Data

Ike, Nobutaka.
  Japan: the new superstate.

  Reprint of the 1973 ed. published by Stanford Alumni
Association, Stanford, Calif., in series:
The Portable Stanford.
  Bibliography: p.
  1. Gross national product—Japan. 2. Japan—Eco-
nomic conditions—1945-   3. Japan—Politics and
government—1945-   4. Japan—Foreign relations.
I. Title.
HC465.I5I38   338′.0952   74-6290
ISBN 0-7167-0767-5
ISBN 0-7167-0766-7 (pbk.)

Printed in the United States of America

1 2 3 4 5 6 7 8 9

This book was published
originally as a part of
The Portable Stanford,
a series of books published by
the Stanford Alumni Association.

CONTENTS

ILLUSTRATIONS

The remaining illustrations are reprinted from *Graphis*, No. 138-139, 1968,
Volume 24, with the gracious permission of Bijutsu Shuppan-sha Publishers, Tokyo.

Illustrations were researched with the gracious cooperation of the Stanford
University Art Library.

PREFACE

The purpose of this book is to try to explain the Japanese "miracle." During the 1960s, the Japanese managed to sustain an economic growth rate that was consistently the highest of all the industrialized nations, with the result that Japan managed to attain third rank in the world in terms of its Gross National Product. There are a number of factors—historical, cultural, social, and economic—that account for this remarkable achievement, and I have tried to delineate these factors and to show how they are interrelated. Success does not come entirely without cost, however, so it is also necessary to take note of the negative aspects of Japan's growth. Pollution is one obvious consequence, but there are other costs—for example, individual and social tensions—and I have also commented on these aspects of contemporary Japanese life.

Does the success of the past necessarily guarantee that the future will be equally bright? Despite optimistic predictions about Japan's future that have been made by some American writers, a number of conditions in Japan lead me to doubt the ability of the Japanese people to sustain the economic growth they have achieved so far. Among these conditions is the problem of access to vital raw materials, especially fossil fuels. In other areas of Japanese life the optimism is quite justifiable. On political and military matters, I am optimistic, for reasons given in the book, about the viability of parliamentary democracy in Japan and about the persistence of the peaceful foreign policy Japan has pursued since 1945.

I am indebted to a number of people for their encouragement, advice, and help with this book. I wish to thank the staff of the Stanford Alumni Association, who published the original edition of the book, for their outstanding art work and editorial assistance. I also wish to acknowledge the help my wife gave me in preparing the manuscript and in reading the galley proofs for that edition.

Stanford, California   *Nobutaka Ike*
March 1974

JAPAN

CHAPTER ONE

PROLOGUE TO MODERNITY

In the beginning, the heaven and earth were formed from chaos, and in the Plain of High Heaven dwelt a multitude of gods. In the fifth generation of these heavenly deities, a brother and sister, Izanagi and Izanami, were born. The celestial pair were united in marriage, and in celebration the other gods gave them a jeweled spear. Standing together on the Heavenly Floating Bridge, they dipped the spear into the ocean below. Sparkling droplets fell from the point of the spear, forming an island.

Izanagi and Izanami descended from the heavens to dwell on the new land. Here Izanami gave birth to the islands of Japan, the mountains, the sea, the rivers, trees, wind and rocks, and to a host of deities. In giving birth to the god of fire, Izanami suffered burns and died.

Her grieving husband followed her to the Land of Darkness and begged her to return: "My beloved spouse, the lands we are creating have not yet been completed; you must come back."

"Wait, my husband," Izanami answered. "I have eaten in the land of the dead and must seek the counsel of the gods of darkness. Turn your eyes from me and wait."

But Izanagi became impatient after the long waiting. He broke a tooth from his comb and set fire to it. As the forbidden light pierced

the caves of the Land of Darkness, his dead wife's corpse decayed
before his eyes.

Terrified by what he had done, Izanagi fled, pursued by the hags
and warriors of the underworld. Izanami, too, followed him, wailing.
At last he escaped from the land of the dead, but he had lost
Izanami forever.

Upon his return to the islands of Japan, Izanagi purified himself
by bathing in a river. As he cast off his jewels and articles of clothing
they were transformed into deities—the Sun Goddess, the Moon
Goddess, the God of Storm, and others. From the Sun Goddess was
descended the first emperor of Japan. He was called Jimmu, or
Divine Valor, and his mission was to unify the islands and all the
peoples of Japan.

As symbols of this divine descent, the sacred mirror, chaplet and
sword, gifts from the Sun Goddess to Jimmu's forefather, have
remained in the keeping of all the emperors of Japan who followed him.

ALTHOUGH JAPAN TODAY is a leading industrial power with strong economic and political ties with the United States, for many Americans it is an enigmatic and mysterious country. The more subtle aspects of Japanese culture seem to have eluded us.

This is a pity, for the two countries are linked by mutual goals and concerns in such a way that what one nation does affects the other. The United States and Japan share similar strategic concerns, as evidenced by a military alliance of many years' standing. The economic bonds between the two countries are also strong: the United States is Japan's best customer, and Japan is the second largest market for American goods and commodities in the world. Both countries are afflicted with similar modern maladies—urban overcrowding, pollution of the environment, a growing fuel shortage, and the problem of waste disposal.

Because of the urgency of these shared interests, it is my belief that for Americans to understand Japan is no longer a luxury but a necessity. Because it is a country whose history and traditions differ greatly from ours, developing this understanding does require some effort. This book rests on the assumption that it is possible to explain the nuances of Japanese culture by examining Japan's unique historical, social, and economic heritage, and by holding a mirror to Japan today.

The myth of the creation and founding of Japan which introduced this chapter expresses some of the enduring beliefs and assumptions which have influenced the development of the Japanese people. Shinto, or Way of the Gods, the indigenous religion derived from Japanese mythology, has had as profound an influence on the Japanese as Christianity has had on the Western world. Much of Shinto belief is expressed by the symbols, moral lessons, and disguised history of the creation myth.

According to Shinto, the gods, man, and nature were born of the same source and are therefore kin. Rather than a sharp division between God and man as seen in Christianity, Shinto implies a divine-human continuity, and recognizes a multitude of deities. Similarly, these myths have led the Japanese to relate to nature in a profoundly different way than does Western man. The assumptions and tenets of traditional Japanese mythology have had a great effect upon individual behavior, social relations, ethical standards, and political organizations in the country.

Perhaps these influences on Japanese culture and tradition can best be explained by taking a look at Japan's historical development from its beginnings to the present time.

Early History

When compared to other Asian civilizations—the Hindu and Chinese, for example—Japanese civilization is quite young. Geographic factors probably account for this. If we look at a world atlas, or even better a globe, we can see that the Japanese islands lie off the eastern end of the gigantic Euro-Asian continent, forming a cul-de-sac. There are four main islands: Hokkaido in the north; the main island of Honshu; Shikoku, which is separated from the main island by the Inland Sea; and Kyushu, which is to the southwest. Japan's nearest neighbor, Korea, lies roughly 100 miles from northern Kyushu.

Historically, Japan's geographic location has meant that the peoples who came to the islands, carried along in the waves of migration which were part of the vast process which filled up the empty land areas of the earth, could not move on to other areas. They were confined to these islands, for to the east lay the vast Pacific Ocean. Moreover, being far removed from the crossroads of migrations where different civilizations met and interacted, they were free to evolve their own civilization in relative isolation. They were not forced to confront other civilizations or to engage in a contest for survival. Although the Japanese at times have been a seagoing people, establishing settlements as far away as Southeast Asia, for the most part they have remained voluntarily isolated from the rest of the world. To this day they have remained a parochial people, lacking those qualities which would enable them to deal freely and easily with foreigners and to adjust with little difficulty to strange environments and situations. Also, as we have suggested, they came on the world stage relatively late in history. In a sense, Japan represented the last frontier in East Asia.

The first residents of the Japanese islands are believed to have been ancestors of the Ainu, a Stone Age people who must have migrated from northern Asia as late as 5,000 years ago. During the first century A.D., waves of migrations of a more technologically advanced people of Mongoloid stock settled the islands, arriving probably from what are now Siberia and Manchuria via the Korean peninsula. There may also have been some movement of people from the South Pacific and southern China. One deduces this from the structure of Japanese dwellings, which are more suited to the warmer climates, and from Japanese mythology, which is said to be similar to the myths found among the Polynesians. Some scholars believe that the myth of the creation of Japan may have originated in the South Seas.

The migrants to Japan first settled in the southwestern parts of the country, on the island of Kyushu and the southern portions of the main island. Since the earliest extant writings go back only to the eighth century A.D., details of the early history of these settlers escape us. We do deduce that, in the early period, the inhabitants were organized into numerous clans or groups of households claiming descent from a common ancestor, worshipping a common deity, and led by a clan chieftain. From time to time these clans engaged in warfare, and as the population increased there occurred internal migrations northward and eastward into areas around the eastern end of the Inland Sea, near the present-day cities of Osaka and Kyoto. Eventually, one of these groups, the Yamato clan, became militarily and politically powerful enough to exercise hegemony over the others.

Borrowing from the Chinese

At this point in their historical development the Japanese people appear to have felt the need for a more complex social organization and form of government than was afforded by the old clan structure. Beginning in about the seventh century A.D., they turned to their neighbors, the Chinese, whose civilization had attained a remarkably high level of sophistication, and engaged in cultural borrowing on a large scale. They copied the Chinese centralized form of government based on the emperor or Son of Heaven, and an imperial bureaucracy whose members were chosen on the basis of competitive civil service examinations. In the process, the chief of the dominant Yamato clan was elevated to the position of emperor, and the Yamato clan god, the Sun Goddess, was designated a national deity.

At the same time, the myths and legends associated with the Yamato clan became the myths of the Japanese nation. The epic of the creation of Japan is derived from this clan myth. No doubt this account, by "explaining" the origins of the imperial family and the divine ancestry of the emperor, served to rationalize the authority of the emperor and to provide a focal point for political loyalty. But in later periods the myth created problems when some authorities insisted on treating it as historical truth rather than legend.

Along with a new form of government, the Japanese also borrowed a new religion, Buddhism, from the Chinese. The introduction of Buddhism owed much to the efforts of the newly created imperial court and the aristocracy associated with it. The most notable early manifestation of the influence of this new religion occurred in architecture and in the visual arts. There was an outburst of temple building, and examples of magnificent temple architecture may be seen even today in Kyoto. Buddhism also stimulated the development of sculpture and the creation of the large wooden figures with fierce countenances which guard the entrances to the temples. Eventually, Buddhism filtered down to the masses where it took root. In the judgment of one astute observer, Shuichi Kato, "Buddhism did not really change the Japanese masses, but the Japanese masses changed Buddhism." (In S. Kato, *Form, Style, Tradition: Reflections on Japanese Art and Society*, Berkeley: University of California Press, 1971.)

Buddhism did not drive out the indigenous Shinto religion. Through the centuries the two religions have managed to coexist in a remarkable way. Shinto, as we have seen from Japanese mythology, states that divine spirits reside in all things, animate and inanimate. Shinto religious practice, therefore, involves the invocation and worship of these spirits in the hope they will exert benevolent influences on one's daily life. Buddhism, by contrast, teaches that individuals cannot escape *karma* or the transmigration of souls. Thus one's fate in this world was determined by his behavior in his previous incarnation, and his fate in the next world will be determined by what he does in this one. A good deal of popular Japanese Buddhism, however, involves prayer and exorcism aimed at securing benefits and wealth in this world and the next, and so in some ways it resembles Shinto practice. In terms of theology, too, the two religions have fused to some extent. It was argued as early as the ninth and tenth centuries that the Japanese gods depicted in mythology were actually local manifestations of Buddhist deities.

Today, according to Japanese government statistics, about seventy million Japanese believe in Shinto and almost eighty million consider themselves to be Buddhists. Since the total population of Japan is only slightly more than 100 million, obviously many millions follow both religions. Traditionally, people have turned to Shinto to bring them good fortune, as it is concerned with the here and now. Most people are married in Shinto ceremonies, for instance. Buddhism, by contrast, is concerned with the hereafter, so it has been the custom for people to turn to Buddhist priests to conduct funeral services.

The ability of Buddhism and Shinto to accommodate each other points up an interesting aspect of the Japanese approach to values. Traditionally, most Japanese have not felt comfortable with an absolute system of values derived from faith in an absolute being. When such systems as Christianity and Communism, for instance, are introduced into Japan, they do not spread, but tend to be confined to small groups. Christianity was first introduced during the sixteenth century, was persecuted and driven underground during the Tokugawa period (1603-1868), and was finally legalized during the Meiji period (1868-1912). So it has a long history; yet the number of Christian converts to this day is quite small, probably numbering less than one in every hundred persons.

One consequence of the Japanese rejection of an absolute system of values is that the culture is hospitable to the introduction of foreign ideas. An individual who believes that nothing is absolute and everything is relative can be pragmatic and believe in things that logically may seem quite contradictory.

The third area of Japanese culture affected by the large-scale importation of Chinese civilization was the written language. As late as the sixth century A.D., the Japanese had not devised a method of writing their language. Although they were apparently aware of the alphabetic forms of writing which had spread into Asia from the Middle East, they chose to borrow the Chinese ideographs, probably because they were then engaged in a wholesale borrowing of things Chinese. But it so happens that Chinese and Japanese are quite different languages, with Japanese being more closely related to Korean, Manchu, Mongolian, and Turkish. The adoption of the Chinese form of writing, thus, was not a happy choice. To this day the language remains cumbersome and difficult to learn, even for Japanese school children, to say nothing of foreigners. The abstruseness of the language certainly has not helped the Japanese make their culture easily accessible to other peoples.

It would be well at this point to return to a consideration of the fate of the political institutions copied from China. As we have noted, the leading clan chieftain became the emperor, and a capital city, laid out neatly in Chinese style, was built to house the imperial court. Those associated with the court became the aristocracy, and with the passage of time there developed a court culture of considerable sophistication.

The aristocracy supported the construction of Buddhist temples and generally contributed to the advancement of art and literature. The courtiers also appear to have spent a good deal of time pursuing their lady friends and composing love poems. We can gain some insight into the urbane life of the court from *The Tale of Genji*, a novel written by Lady Murasaki, who was a servant to the Empress Akiko in the eleventh century. A work considered to be the world's first novel, it has been admirably translated into English by Arthur Waley.

Not all political institutions and practices adopted from the Chinese culture survived in their original forms. For instance, the Chinese system of recruiting the civil service on the basis of competitive examinations fell by the wayside because the Japanese limited the eligibles to a small class of aristocrats. Moreover, the ownership of arable land was initially legally vested in the emperor, who was to apportion it among the peasants according to family size. From time to time, land was supposed to be reallocated in order to ensure equitable distribution. In return, farmers assumed the obligation to pay taxes to the imperial treasury in the form of farm produce and labor.

As the population grew, more and more land was needed to be brought under cultivation. To achieve this, intermittent military campaigns were launched against the Ainu during the eighth and ninth centuries to push the frontier ever northward and put more land under the control of the emperor. Many Ainu were killed during these campaigns, and others were assimilated into the dominant culture. Today, the few surviving Ainu live mostly in Hokkaido, the northernmost island, where they are considered a tourist attraction. Ainu influence is evident in some place names in the islands. Fuji, the name of Japan's most popular mountain, is one example. The Ainu heritage is also indicated in those Japanese who have relatively heavy hair growth on their faces and bodies.

In fighting the Ainu, most of the aristocrats were loath to exchange the pleasant life of the court for the rigors of the frontier, so they sent their younger brothers or sons north to "pacify the barbarians." A parallel development was the gradual breakdown of the government machinery. Cultivators were supposed to pay taxes on the land they tilled, but various tax-dodging devices came into use, with the result that the flow of revenue into the imperial treasury dwindled over time. By contrast, those who had gone out into the frontier areas gained control of more and more land. The government, weakened by its shrinking tax base, could no longer enforce its will and maintain order throughout the country. In this situation, what the central government lost, the up-and-coming land-owning families in the frontier provinces

gained. The latter began to recruit private armies to protect their domains, thus providing the basis for the eventual development of the samurai or warrior class and a political order based on feudalism.

The Shift to Feudalism

The establishment of a military government in Kamakura (at present a fashionable suburb of Tokyo and the location of a gigantic, world-renowned statue of Buddha) in 1185 marked the formal beginning of the feudal period. In the shift toward the feudal system, the imperial family was rendered politically impotent. Actually, there have been periods in Japanese history when the emperor was not only powerless but impecunious. There are said to have been occasions when an emperor who died could not be buried because the imperial family could not afford the burial expenses. But despite the weakening influence of the emperor, the sovereign institution survived; the ruler's stamp of approval was required before any military leader, however powerful, could claim that his regime was legal.

Japanese feudalism, like feudalism in other lands, was characterized by a tendency toward chronic warfare. Feudal barons skilled in the art of warfare and endowed with superb leadership qualities managed to bring numerous samurai and large tracts of farm land under their control, only to be overcome by rival barons a few years later. At one time two proud and powerful families fought it out for survival, a situation similar to the Wars of the Roses in British history.

It was not until the sixteenth century that the process of political disintegration had run its course, resulting in the emergence of a countercycle leading to the reestablishment of central authority. Three illustrious military leaders were associated with this process of military unification, each carrying on where his predecessor had left off. The first of the triumvirate was Nobunaga Oda (1534-82), who established himself in central Japan through a series of brilliant military campaigns. At the age of forty-nine Nobunaga was wounded by a force commanded by one of his vassal barons and, seeing the hopelessness of his situation, he committed suicide by setting fire to the temple where he was staying.

Nobunaga was succeeded by his leading general, Hideyoshi Toyotomi (1536-98), a man who overcame his humble peasant origins to become a great military leader. In 1592, Hideyoshi invaded Korea, apparently as part of a larger plan to conquer China.

The third leader, Iyeyasu Tokugawa (1542-1616), took over after Hideyoshi's death and carried the process of centralization to fruition when he won a decisive victory against a coalition of rivals in 1600, thereby establishing himself as the strongest military leader in all Japan. It is common in Japan to cite three couplets to show the different temperaments of these military leaders:

> NOBUNAGA: *"I'll kill the cuckoo if it won't sing."*
>
> HIDEYOSHI: *"I'll try to make the cuckoo sing."*
>
> IYEYASU: *"I'll wait until the cuckoo sings."*

By virtue of his victory, in 1603 Iyeyasu assumed the title of *Sei-i-tai Shogun*, or "Barbarian-quelling Generalissimo," a rank bestowed upon him by the emperor, and established his headquarters in Edo, a swampy stretch of land which ultimately became the largest city in the world, Tokyo.

The Tokugawa Heritage

Having risen to power after a long period of civil wars in which numerous military leaders had come and gone with remarkable rapidity, the first Tokugawa ruler was determined to found a dynasty that would survive for many generations to come. To achieve this stability, he and his advisors adopted the strategy of freezing the status quo. Their aim was not to encourage innovation, change, and progress, but to preserve the society and culture as they were at the beginning of the seventeenth century.

Toward that end, the Tokugawa Shogun worked out a series of ingenious institutional devices. The Tokugawa house directly governed about one-fourth of the country, with the remainder parceled out among several hundred feudal nobles. Some of these nobles were faithful allies, but others were defeated rivals whom the Shogun considered to be untrustworthy. The allies were brought into the Tokugawa administration, while the rivals were excluded. Moreover, the Shogun went to considerable pains to make certain that no rival feudal baron or coalition could threaten his hard-earned hegemony. Here we will cite only a few of his more notable schemes by way of illustration.

The Tokugawa Shogun insisted that plans for all new castles and fortifications be submitted to the Tokugawa government for approval. He also made use of political spies to find out what potential rivals were doing. The imperial court, which remained in the traditional capital of Kyoto, was isolated from politics, and feudal barons were prohibited from approaching the emperor directly. The Tokugawa Shogun also instituted a system of "alternative attendance," whereby all feudal lords were required to spend a certain amount of time every year in residence in Edo under the watchful eye of the Shogun and his officials. When the feudal baron returned to his home to look after the affairs of his own domain, he was forced to leave his family behind as hostages. A practical consequence of this sort of arrangement was the stimulation of trade. The comings and goings of feudal nobles accompanied by their large retinues of bodyguards, servants, and luggage bearers encouraged the establishment of inns and other business establishments along the main routes of travel. Finally, another device that had profound effects in the long run was the forcible closing of the country to all foreign commerce and contacts. This was decreed in 1638 during the reign of the grandson of the founder of the Tokugawa dynasty.

A Period of Isolation

One of the reasons for the closing of the country was the spread of Christianity resulting from the activities of Jesuit and Franciscan missionaries who came by sea from Portugal beginning in the mid-sixteenth century. By 1615 these missionaries had converted some 300,000 Japanese to Christianity. In the eyes of many officials, Christianity, with its allegiance to a foreign god, was a subversive doctrine and Christian converts were considered potential traitors to their country. Japanese leaders felt Christian converts might put loyalty to the church, which was headquartered in Europe, over loyalty to their feudal lords. They looked upon converts as a potential fifth column. Another and perhaps more important reason for the suspicion the Tokugawa house felt toward the converts was the Shogun's fear that one or more of his rival barons might form an alliance with a European power and attempt to overthrow his government.

A rebellion of Christian converts, most of whom were oppressed peasants living on the island of Kyushu, in 1637 and 1638 precipitated the closing of the country. More than 30,000 rebels held out for nearly three months against a military force sent to put them down. The rebellion did not end until virtually all the defending Christians were killed.

After this incident, the Tokugawa banned all overseas trade. The Dutch, who were not Catholic, were allowed to maintain a small trading station in Nagasaki, which had developed into an important port with the coming of the Portuguese missionaries and traders, under limited conditions. An occasional Chinese trading mission was allowed into the country, but otherwise the Japanese were compelled, by their

own choice, to live upon their own resources, both in terms of economic needs and scientific and technological knowledge. Everything considered, they managed reasonably well. Over the years, the hardworking and frugal peasants were able to increase the production of food and other farm commodities so that mass starvation did not occur. But it is also worth noting that eventually the population stabilized somewhere between twenty-seven and thirty million. This was achieved through openly practiced abortion and through infanticide, which was referred to as *mabiki*, a term also used to indicate the thinning out of young shoots in a newly seeded field.

In the area of science and technology, the effects of national isolation were more severe. Those intellectuals who took the trouble to learn to read Dutch could, after a fashion, find out what was happening in Europe, but at best the Dutch trading station served only as a tiny window on the world. It was no substitute for more open, direct, and frequent contact with Europe. Consequently, Tokugawa Japan was unable to profit in any significant way from the scientific and technological advances which accompanied the industrial revolution in Europe. To the best of our knowledge, even as late as 1850 the Japanese had not reached the point of development where they were able to build factories which harnessed the steam engine to productive use.

Another important consequence of Tokugawa hegemony and the policy of national isolation was the coming of a prolonged era of peace. After a period of chronic civil wars, a pax Tokugawa descended upon the land. To be sure, the price of peace was an oppressive and heavy-handed rule by the feudal authorities, but at least the slaughter of innocent people had ceased. Moreover, the country was not involved in foreign wars; no country threatened the Japanese, and they engaged in no aggressive actions abroad. War disappeared from the Japanese scene for a period of more than 250 years, a phenomenon few countries have experienced in modern times.

Peace brought important dividends. In the economic field, commerce and the handicraft industry enjoyed growth. Regional specialization developed, so that one area became known for its paper, another for its dyestuffs, still another for its textiles. Goods were shipped from one part of the country to another in small coastal sailing vessels. The existence of commodity exchanges in commercial centers suggests that the economy had reached a high level of complexity. For example, trading in futures of rice, the most important staple crop, was permitted in Osaka in western Japan.

In this environment of vigorous trade and production, the merchant class, which evolved from tradespeople living in the larger cities, prospered. Merchants, dedicated to making money and spending it, developed their own subculture, and their tastes influenced the art and literature of the time. The Kabuki theater flourished, thanks to the merchant patronage it enjoyed. The origin of the Kabuki dramatic form is somewhat obscure, but it evidently evolved from the classical Nō drama and the puppet theater. Although Kabuki used traditional themes from mythology, episodes from court life, and historical accounts of warfare as subject matter, it departed from customary theatrical forms. It featured robust movement, swordplay, flamboyant gestures, and even eroticism—all features demanded by merchant audiences bent on being amused and thrilled. The *haiku*, a form of short poem, and a technique of wood-block printing which made it possible to mass-produce artwork, were other products of merchant life which remain popular to this day.

Despite the wealth it managed to amass, the Japanese merchant class, unlike the European bourgeoisie, never felt strong enough nor sufficiently independent to challenge the political power of the feudal nobility. For one thing, the merchants became associated with the establishment to some extent, as they were creditors to the feudal nobles and the samurai. Moreover, the line separating the merchant class from the samurai became blurred as some merchants were able to buy quasi-samurai status, and some samurai abandoned their calling, which was not very lucrative, and became peasants or merchants. But perhaps the most important reason for the timidity of the merchant class was the inability to exploit overseas markets because of the isolationist policy of the Tokugawa regime. The domestic market was too restricted to encourage the emergence of the sort of innovative, daring, and aggressive entrepreneur who would be anxious to break the confining bonds of a feudal system.

Prolonged peace also affected the warrior class. Those whose profession is warfare flourish in situations where there are frequent opportunities to perform acts of heroism. There is nothing like combat duty to speed up promotions. But a specialized hereditary warrior class in an era of prolonged peace represented an anomaly of serious proportions. The samurai were supposed to maintain their martial skills, and *bushido*, or the code of the warrior, which stressed loyalty and readiness to die nobly, reached its highest level of articulation during this period. But there were no more wars. Gradually the samurai moved into castle towns, the headquarters of their feudal masters, and settled into a sort of parasitic life, living off rice stipends paid them from the lord's treasury. Many of those in the lower income levels became indebted to moneylenders and were compelled to live a life of poverty.

According to a folk-saying of the period, even though the samurai were too poor to eat, out of pride they would go around with toothpicks in their mouths.

Probably in order to keep them occupied, the regime encouraged samurai to devote themselves to learning, and toward that end schools were established and maintained by the feudal government. These schools stressed Confucian principles. Originally, Confucianism was introduced into Japan during the seventh century, coming from China along with Buddhism. It spread gradually, especially among the warrior class. During the Tokugawa period Confucianism served to rationalize the existing social order, which was based on a sharply defined series of social classes—warriors, peasants, artisans, and merchants. Confucianism set as its goal a harmonious social order achieved by a set of rulers who governed by setting the proper moral example for the people. It envisioned a hierarchical society in which each member performed in accordance with his allocated station in life. Since Tokugawa feudalism depended on personal loyalties for its survival, it made sense to adopt as orthodoxy a philosophy which advocated this sort of moral code. Confucianism was at first closely associated with the elite warrior class, but it eventually filtered down to the masses. Certain Confucian notions, such as respect for filial piety and social hierarchy, persist even today.

Some of the more talented and ambitious graduates of the Confucian schools were able to apply their learning by securing positions in the various feudal governments. In the absence of war, bureaucratic achievement represented one of the few avenues of advancement open to the samurai. Able administrators could increase their hereditary stipends. Given the fairly large number of feudal jurisdictions, there was room for a substantial number of administrators. But clearly these jobs were available to only a small percentage of the samurai, who comprised something like 5 percent of the total population.

The promotion of education among the samurai appears to have rubbed off on the common people. Schools for commoners were established in many Buddhist temples, and sons of the more affluent non-samurai families were able to attend. Eventually education became further diffused, and by 1850 as many as one-half of the adult males could read and write. Even today, many countries cannot claim as high a literacy rate.

Economic expansion and the spread of education obviously must be put into the plus column, but there were also some minuses in the picture. The economic difficulties which plagued many members of the samurai class have already been mentioned. One of the causes of the impoverishment of the samurai was undoubtedly the inability of the feudal governments to manage their finances. Governments seem to have a tendency to spend more money than they collect. In Tokugawa Japan, many feudal nobles, unable to balance their budgets, resorted to measures which have a familiar ring. One method was to debase the currency. Gold and silver coins in circulation were called in and melted down. By reproducing many smaller coins with the same face value the authorities were able to make a tidy profit. Of course, before long price levels rose to reflect the debasement, so this was not a permanent solution. Another method was to borrow money. But these were the days before bond markets and federal reserve systems had been invented, so the feudal authorities went to those who had the money—the merchants. Because the barons had political power and the merchants did not, the latter found it difficult to refuse requests for loans. But, over the long run, those barons who became known as credit risks found that loans became more and more difficult to come by. Finally, some of the nobles took to "borrowing" from their samurai retainers by reducing their stipends, a measure which is unlikely to have aroused much enthusiasm on the part of the warrior class.

There were other indications that all was not well. Although there are signs that agricultural production in the aggregate probably increased, it is doubtful that farmers as a group were affluent. A folk-saying of the period likened peasants to sesame seeds, a source of oil: "The harder you squeeze the peasants, the more you get out of them." When pushed too far by rapacious tax collectors or grasping money-lenders, they revolted. In some revolts, a few angry farmers—armed with pitchforks, bamboo spears, and other weapons—would set fire to the house of the village moneylender in an effort to burn the mortgages and promissory notes within; other revolts were much larger in scale and involved thousands of rioters. Historians have compiled long lists of peasant revolts, and the lists are growing as more documents are discovered in local archives and family records.

In time other indicators of unrest appeared. Beginning in the eighteenth century, scholars studying earlier Japanese history began to question the legitimacy of Tokugawa rule and to suggest obliquely that the imperial house should be the focus of political loyalty. Other groups of scholars devoted themselves to the so-called "Dutch studies," which they saw as an avenue of learning more about what was going on in Europe. In the intellectual world, too, attitudes had changed in the course of Tokugawa rule.

Perhaps it would be well at this point in the narrative to assess the events of the Tokugawa period and to suggest implications for sub-

彼理ノ子
なをオリイル。ス。ト

セ。ト。ニ。や。
船将アフ。ホット
二月十五日献員文之助
へ。り。代り上陸
白髪手宴織
頼本朝人。

ペ。り。
船将アフ。ホット

一近習言
ポ。ッ。テ。ノ。レ

sequent developments. Quite clearly, the Tokugawa leaders did not succeed in perpetuating the status quo by putting a lid on all forms of social change. Although the pace was slow, change did occur. Some of the changes—economic growth and educational progress, for instance —were beneficial, but there were also symptoms of stress: governmental deficits, peasant unrest, and intellectual ferment. Still, the Tokugawa system endured for more than 250 years, not an inconsequential span of history. How much longer it could have persisted without a breakdown is hard to say.

In the last analysis, this is an academic question, for by the end of the eighteenth century continued national isolation became impossible. Japan's geographic remoteness from the growing centers of world power in Europe had enabled her to remain isolated; however, the industrial revolution, which produced not only the steamship, but a rising business class restless in its search for profit, prestige, and power, changed the picture drastically. Moreover, the rise of the United States to the position of a Pacific power added to the pressures on Japan. The immediate American interest in opening up Japan was to find ports accessible to whaling ships needing water, provisions, and a safe haven from Pacific storms, and to find coaling stations for steamships, which were being used increasingly in international trade.

The End of Isolationism

Because Commodore Matthew Perry's name is prominently associated with the opening of Japan, Americans tend to overlook the contributions of others. Actually, Perry was in a position to achieve a breakthrough, to "open" Japan's closed doors, because the ground had been prepared. From about 1790 on, vessels representing a variety of nations—Great Britain, France, and Russia, as well as the United States—sailed into Japanese ports seeking to persuade the Japanese to change their isolationist policy. The captains and crews of these vessels were treated politely, given water and provisions, and told firmly to go away. Seen from the Japanese perspective, Perry's mission in 1853 represented the culmination of a process which had begun long before, for powerful seagoing nations had been making tentative landings for some fifty years. Also, a small group of Japanese who made an attempt to keep abreast of international affairs learned that the Chinese had suffered a humiliating defeat by British forces in the Opium War of 1839-42. Fearing their isolationism might place them in a defenseless position, some of the more realistic Japanese leaders came to the conclusion that the times called for a fundamental change in national policy.

This change was not easily accomplished. The situation called for strong, decisive, and innovative leadership, and in the end the Tokugawa house, weakened by internal dissent, financial difficulties, and ebbing inner vitality, could not rise to meet the challenge. 'Indecision at the top in turn encouraged potential rivals to agitate and conspire to overthrow the Tokugawa house. This sort of situation provides the makings of a variegated and fascinating panorama of political history, and the fall of Tokugawa Japan was no exception. The story, which would require nothing less than a large volume to tell, is obviously beyond the scope of this book. All we can do here is summarize the main historical tendencies in broad strokes, omitting much of the color and sense of excitement.

First, most of the leaders felt that the international environment was a hostile one, that national security was threatened, and that there was a need to strengthen military defenses.

Second, the feudal nobles and their samurai advisors were divided on the question of whether or not Japan should abandon the time-honored policy of national isolation.

Third, a vague feeling of doubt about the viability of feudalism and the form of government headed by the Tokugawa Shogun began to surface. Although it was not clearly articulated by any one individual or group, the historical situation called for a daring leap forward in a new direction rather than continued incremental change along a well-worn track. Such a leap finally came after a protracted period of pulling and hauling between those in the center of the political stage and the contenders coming in from the wings. This was the Meiji Restoration of 1868.

What happened from a narrow legal standpoint was the resignation of the Tokugawa Shogun and the "restoration" of the authority of the sixteen-year-old emperor, whose reign was designated "Meiji," or "Enlightened Rule." But the Meiji Restoration represented much more than a changing of the palace guard. To be sure, it was nothing so sweeping and fundamental as the French or Bolshevik revolutions. Rather, it might be characterized as a revolution from above led by a coalition of young samurai, drawn largely from the feudal domains which had been traditionally hostile to the Tokugawa house, and dissatisfied nobles, drawn from the imperial court. As often happens in instances of this kind, political change did lead to some violence; a civil war broke out in January 1868 between the supporters of the new regime and remnants of the Tokugawa forces. But the hostilities, which lasted several months, were not followed by a bloodbath. Members of the Tokugawa family were eventually given titles and made part of a new nobility. Still, it should be stressed that the Restoration ushered in a series of reforms which modernized the political and social character of Japan.

The Meiji Reforms

One way to characterize briefly what happened in the decades after the Restoration of 1868 is to take note of the slogan of the period: "Rich country, strong army." First let us examine the concept of "rich country." Japan's leaders compared their country with the more advanced nations of Europe and with the United States and saw that it was backward and poor. So, just as their ancestors had turned to China, these leaders actively imported Western technology and institutions. Numerous foreign experts were hired to come to Japan and teach their skills, and large numbers of Japanese students were sent to study in European and American schools at the expense of the Japanese government. The government set up model factories to encourage Japanese entrepreneurs to start up new industries and, in some instances, the government itself established and operated factories, which were later sold to private interests. During this period Japanese entrepreneurs came from samurai, merchant, and landlord classes. A few did unusually well, and the firms they founded eventually developed into the huge and powerful industrial combines known as the *zaibatsu* (literally, "money clique"). They had key political connections which enabled them to secure lucrative subsidies and to buy government enterprises at bargain prices.

A program of industrialization cannot be sustained without supporting structures, and so attention was also paid to other sectors. From the beginning, the Meiji leaders established a system of mass education. Based on American and, later, German models, the new educational system led to a high rate of literacy among the people. A banking system copied from the West was also inaugurated, as well as a modern transportation system based on an extensive network of railroads and several steamship lines.

In the social field, the old feudal system was abolished, the legal distinction between the samurai and the common people was done away with, and the dispossessed samurai were encouraged to take up useful occupations. To ease their transition into civilian life, the samurai were granted pensions in lieu of their stipends. Later, when the government discovered that the pension system was too costly, they were given settlements in lump sums.

The other half of the Meiji slogan, "strong army," refers to the problem of national security. Partly because they were mostly of samurai origin, and partly because the opening of their country took place under an implied threat of American force, the leaders of Meiji Japan placed great importance on military matters. They were determined that their country should become strong militarily because they perceived the world to be made up of nations with an aggressive bent. Japanese leaders of the period wanted more than security; they set as a national goal the achievement of equality with the most advanced nations of the Western world. Toward the end of the nineteenth century, Prince Ito, a leading statesman, said that his country's aim was to secure "prosperity, strength, and culture, and consequent recognized status of membership upon an equal footing in the family of the most powerful and civilized nations of the world." It is worth noting that this drive to catch up with and even to surpass the Western nations still persists. One finds it hard to imagine a Gallup poll on whether or not Americans were superior to other nationalities, but Japanese pollsters often ask this sort of question of their respondents. And over the years, more and more Japanese think they are superior.

The Japanese concern with national security and the drive to achieve equality were factors which led to the early appearance of an imperialistic foreign policy. In the late nineteenth century it was said that the sun never set on the British Empire, and even the smaller European nations had acquired colonies in Asia and Africa. Perceiving the possession of colonial empires to be the hallmark of a Great Power, the Japanese began to reach beyond the boundaries of their islands. The Marxist argument that imperialism represents the last stage of capitalism, motivated by a need to seek foreign outlets for surplus capital, would not apply in the case of Japan's drive to acquire possessions. Even as early as the 1880s, when the country was still in the process of modernization, the Japanese were engaged in a dispute with the Chinese imperial government over who should control Korea, which had traditionally been under Chinese tutelage. Eventually this dispute led to the Sino-Japanese War of 1894-95. Japan's victory assured her of a foothold in Korea and led to the annexation of Formosa, which she held until 1945.

Japanese moves to gain influence on the Asian continent soon resulted in conflict with Tsarist Russia, which had designs on Manchuria as well as Korea. The result was the Russo-Japanese War of 1904-05, which Japan won by a narrow margin. Victory enabled Japan to annex Korea in 1910 and to extend her influence into Manchuria through the acquisition of the South Manchurian Railway. One could think of a situation where, at an earlier stage, Japan might have thrown in her lot with fellow Asians and become the leader of a coalition of

Asian countries against the West. But the motives for modernization mitigated against such a course, and Japan ended up essentially making common cause with the Western nations. It is worth noting, in this connection, that even today most Japanese tend to identify with the West rather than with Asia, even though geographically, racially, and culturally they are more oriental than occidental.

In the year 1912, the Emperor Meiji died. During his lifetime Japan had emerged from feudalism and transformed itself into a modern nation. According to the standards which prevailed at the time in the world community, the Japanese had arrived. No other Asian country had managed to duplicate the growth of the Japanese empire during the forty-four-year span of the Meiji period. This achievement can be attributed to a number of factors, including the quality of leadership, the willingness of the masses to work hard, and the country's openness to cultural borrowing. But it is useful to remember that the Japanese had entered the phase of rapid modernization relatively well-equipped to manage multi-dimensional change. Stated in another way, the Tokugawa heritage had prepared them well.

Although a sense of regionalism expressed in the use of local dialects and adherence to local customs persisted, there was no problem of national identity. A widely shared commitment to a set of values, a way of life, and to the nation created strong bonds among the people. In this sense, Japan was fortunate; unlike many of today's developing countries, Japan was not subject to religious, linguistic, and racial tensions and rivalries. Another asset was the governmental bureaucracy developed during the Tokugawa period, which served as a model for bureaucratic management. We have already catalogued the more important types of change which were promoted by the government during the Meiji period. When we refer to the government, we mean the actions of this bureaucracy. In fact, we may find in Meiji Japan the first instance of a modernizing bureaucracy in action.

Finally, the feudal heritage of Tokugawa Japan appears to have been of considerable significance during the decades of modernization. Western history suggests that the transition to a modern nation is probably easier to make from feudalism than, say, from an autocratic centralized empire. Although the reasons for this are not exactly clear, two factors seem to be operating. First, since feudalism is by definition decentralized, there are several or more power centers, rather than the one which exists in an empire. The probability of one of the centers making a successful response to a crisis situation is higher. By contrast, if a centralized empire fails to make a successful transition to a new form of society and government, all is lost. Second, feudalism enjoys a high quotient of political loyalty. Because it must involve change affecting various sectors of society, modernization is necessarily a destabilizing process. A strong sense of political loyalty can serve as a countervailing force against tendencies toward dissention and conflict.

So far we have stressed the positive aspects of Japan's response to the Western impact and the program of modernization which followed. But we should also remember that there is often a price to be paid for advantages gained. The negative consequences of Japan's quest for modernity should not be glossed over. Stated baldly, the price was severe restriction upon the right to undertake free intellectual inquiry, to speak one's mind openly, and to engage in political dissent. The Constitution, ostensibly a gift to the people from the emperor in 1889, established a parliamentary form of government and enunciated an extended list of civil liberties. In practice, however, the government never operated quite like the liberal Western governments upon which it was partially modeled.

The Constitution of 1889 represented a compromise between traditional political theory on the one hand, and Western ideals of democracy and individualism on the other. Although the leaders encouraged large-scale importation of Western civilization, especially in the areas of technology and science, they were not quite ready to encourage the adoption of liberal political and social concepts. Many intellectuals would have preferred a more thoroughgoing form of Westernization, but they were without sufficient political clout to achieve it. As a consequence, they adopted an anti-Establishment stance which has continued into the present. They were not particularly enamored of the official theory of state, the principle of *kokutai*, which is written with two ideographs meaning "country" and "body." *Kokutai* represented an organic conception of state in which the state was seen as making up a body. Specifically, the theory stated that the Japanese state was unique in the world in that it was founded by the first emperor, who was directly descended from the Sun Goddess, and composed of his subjects, who were regarded as his children. Stated in another way, the Japanese state was one large family headed by a patriarch, the emperor. This principle, if accepted, made political loyalty identical with filial piety.

Logically, this theory made the emperor the supreme political leader, but in actual practice he reigned but did not rule. His subjects were supposed to advise and assist him in making political decisions which were carried out in the form of ordinances and laws issued in his name. One of the bodies which advised him was the parliament, but there were many others, some defined in the Constitution, others not. An important set of advisors were those connected with the armed forces.

The army and navy jealously guarded the principle of the "independence of the Supreme Command," which made them the sole advisors on matters relating to military and defense affairs. The army and navy chiefs of staff had the power to report directly to the emperor, bypassing the prime minister and other government leaders. Clearly, the generals and admirals occupied a privileged position within the governmental structure, and they utilized this position to gain considerable control over the government.

As can be inferred, the system of government articulated in the Constitution represented a compromise between Western forms and the doctrine of direct imperial rule. A certain amount of tension inherent in the system became more serious with the passage of time. By the early 1920s industrial development had produced a working class in the big cities, while the spread of education and literacy had stimulated the growth of urban newspapers and other forms of mass communication. The result was increased demand for more opportunities to participate in political affairs. At times, during the 1920s, the political parties were able to gain control of the government and it appeared that Western-style parliamentary government based on majorities in the House of Representatives might become the norm. The worldwide economic depression of the 1930s, however, aborted the trend toward political democracy. Declining prices for agricultural produce brought distress to the peasants, while unemployment and widespread bankruptcy struck the cities.

In many parts of the world the crisis atmosphere of the early 1930s gave rise to dictatorships, and in Japan the armed forces, especially the army, gradually came to dominate the government. During this period of military rule Japan pursued an aggressive expansionist foreign policy, leading to the occupation of vast areas of the Chinese mainland and to an eventual confrontation with the Great Powers. In domestic politics, the rise of the military to power led to increasingly stringent censorship of publications and thought control.

Even so-called liberal professors were hounded and some were driven from their academic positions. A celebrated case involved Professor Tatsukichi Minobe, an authority on the Constitution who incurred the displeasure of ultra-nationalists, self-proclaimed patriots, and militarists for having argued that the emperor was an "organ" of the state, thereby contravening the more orthodox view that the emperor *was* the state. In 1935, Minobe found himself at the vortex of a national controversy and was forced to retire in disgrace. His case is one of many which have led Japanese intellectuals to refer to this period of their national history as the "dark valley."

One of the notable achievements of the nearly seven years of American occupation which followed World War II was the removal of the heavy hand of government repression. The Japanese government still occasionally engages in what may appear to be a quixotic form of censorship. For instance, the government hires students to black out certain sections of photographs in *Playboy* magazines which are imported into the country. But in general, Japan today cannot be said to be a country which suffers from an excessive degree of repression. Nevertheless, many individuals, especially the intellectuals and those on the Left, fear that the "dark valley" may reappear someday to deprive them of their recently acquired freedom. Even today, the political issues which provoke an emotional response and precipitate political violence generally are connected with the so-called "reverse course" policy—attempts on the part of the conservative government to undo some of the occupation-sponsored reforms and to return to the prewar way of running the government. The buildup of the armed forces, attempts to strengthen the power of the police and to centralize control of the educational system, and similar measures always arouse political passions and provoke heated controversy. To those of us who are onlookers, such a response may seem to smack of paranoia, but those more directly involved feel that the danger is real and even imminent.

Post-1945 Japan

The defeat in 1945 marked a watershed in Japan's modern history. The defeat itself came as a traumatic shock, and since it was unprecedented the people were without guidelines as to how they should respond. Many felt, however, that their leaders had misled them, that perhaps all these years they had believed in the wrong things, and that their collective goals had been misdirected. They were in a mood, therefore, to look critically at the past and to consider moving in new directions.

When the occupation came and ordered a whole series of reforms intended to change the distribution of political power and even to change the fabric of society, many welcomed the reforms instead of resisting them. During the first few years of the occupation, Japan was probably subjected to more Western influence than during the several decades which preceded it. The details of what the occupation tried to do make a fascinating story but, aside from a brief discussion of the economic aspects, the subject is beyond the scope of this book. However, it would be pertinent to make some comments about the effects of the occupation on the Japanese.

Perhaps because of its scope, no one, either American or Japanese, has yet succeeded in making an objective and comprehensive study of the lasting consequences of occupation policy. Those who study Japan sense that, compared to the prewar period, things have changed. The family, for instance, is much less closely knit than it used to be. The sense of individualism has obviously been strengthened and the trend appears to be continuing. Conversely, there appears to be less pressure for social conformity, and Japanese society undoubtedly is more open than it used to be. Perhaps the most marked change has occurred on the political level, particularly in regard to the institutional structure. The electorate has much more say in choosing which leaders shall govern and, in this sense, the government is more responsive to public moods and wishes than it was before the occupation. Political dissent, too, is more tolerated than it was in the past. These are important changes which should not be minimized.

Still, to me, the striking feature of postwar Japan is not that changes have occurred, but the fact that more change has not taken place, given the historical circumstances. In certain fundamental respects there is a sense of continuity. As we have seen, Japanese society was originally based on a clan structure. This was followed by feudalism, with bands of warriors held together by ideals of personal loyalty. The decline of feudalism, accelerated by the impact of Western influences in the nineteenth century, led to a more modern form of society and polity. In the short span of 100 years, Japan was transformed from a technologically backward, agrarian country into one of the world's greatest industrial powers. The adoption of modern industry and scientific technology, the spread of mass education and urbanization, and the fostering of democracy by the American occupation authorities could conceivably have produced a more individualistically oriented society.

Yet in reality, the fabric of Japanese society, the way in which people relate to each other and to those in positions of authority, has changed at a slow pace. Despite the social leveling which has undoubtedly occurred, the sense of hierarchy and respect for seniority remains strong. Most Japanese value the principle of achievement and are, accordingly, highly competitive. Still, the group is dominant and Japanese society is remarkably structured. There are many paradoxes here. How the resolution of some of these paradoxes—most notably the conflict between cooperation and competition—gives contemporary Japan its dynamic qualities will be the theme of the next chapter.

TWO

JP STRUCTURE: COOPERATION, COMPETITION, AND CONFLICT

As ARISTOTLE NOTED more than 2,000 years ago, no one can live apart from society. Human beings need groups to nurture life, to carry on economic activities, to sustain their spiritual needs, and to continue the species. Groups, as such, are indispensable, and different sorts of groups perform different functions in society. The needs met by the family are different from those met by a professional or neighborhood group, for instance. We are able to shift attachments from one group to another, depending upon our needs.

The element which makes group life possible is cooperation. Members must be willing to give and take. Children being socialized and taught to get along with playmates are admonished that they must "learn to share." Groups could not exist if their members did not share certain values and goals. Groups which achieve effectiveness and unity are sustained by a sense of common interest reinforced by common efforts. For members, successful teamwork can be a satisfying experience.

But there is another side to human beings. Each person is a self-enclosed, self-directing unit. Each individual has some degree of autonomy in addition to thoughts, feelings, and purposes which set him apart from the group. An individual's concern for his interests, his reputation, and his social standing motivate him to compete with others. Somehow, the need to cooperate and the impulse to compete must be reconciled. The problem of adjusting the ego interest and the group interest is universal, and the persistence of conflict in human society suggests that the adjustment is difficult, if not impossible. No formula has yet been found for arriving at a perfect adjustment, but it is clear that different societies tend to deal with the problem by stressing either cooperation or competition.

Groups in Japanese History

At the risk of oversimplification, we should state at the outset that Japanese society, from its earliest history to the present, has emphasized the group rather than the individual. As David Plath, an American anthropologist who has studied Japanese culture, has put it, Japan is a country where the self is underdeveloped and the social order over-developed.

Historically, the first important social groups to emerge in Japan were the clans. By definition, the clan, a group which claims descent from a common ancestor, is based on kinship. Under the control of each clan were groups known as *be*, which were guilds of specialized workers such as farmers, weavers, swordmakers, and scribes, who pursued their occupations generation after generation. With the advent of feudalism the clans and the associated guilds were gradually replaced by groups of warriors. Ambitious samurai attached themselves to feudal nobles and together made war on other bands of warriors. The bond was no longer kinship, but loyalty. In return for the loyalty and service the samurai gave the lords, they received material rewards and security. A Japanese historian commenting on the feudal period has pointed out that both loyalty and filial piety were stressed: a samurai was obligated to be loyal to the lord who gave him his stipend and filial to his ascendants, for he owed his right to the hereditary stipend to the bravery of his father or other ancestors. Incidentally, an important difference between groups based on kinship and feudal groups based on loyalty was that the latter could expand, while the former were inherently limited.

During the Tokugawa period, the warrior class represented a tiny minority of the population. The vast majority of the people were peasants who lived in small villages scattered throughout the islands. In this respect Japanese civilization is similar to other Asian civilizations, which are typically based on villages. By contrast, Western civilization has from its beginnings centered on the city, notable examples of which are Athens and Rome. When compared to cities in Europe, Asian cities are new, many of them having grown since the nineteenth century. Capital cities like Peking, the seat of political authority, are exceptions.

Village life differs from urban life in that it places a premium on cooperation, conformity, and consensus. The reasons for this will become clearer if we look at some of the salient features of life in villages. First, coordinated group effort was required if irrigation was used, as, for example, in the cultivation of rice. To build the network of irrigation canals and to maintain them, community effort was required. Moreover, timing the flow of water and adjusting the rate of flow had to be determined by the whole village. A nonconforming individual who insisted on doing things his own way could wreck the whole enterprise. Second, village life was characterized by a low rate of mobility. Most children born in the village expected to spend their lives there. This meant that everyone knew everybody else in the village, and if one were not able to get along reasonably well with one's relatives and neighbors life could be intolerable. One could not avoid relatives and neighbors by moving to another community. In fact, the severest sanction a village could impose on an errant member was to ostracize him. The villagers would have nothing to do with him, and would not give him aid except in a crisis—if his house was burning or he was dying.

Third, leadership in village affairs was in the hands of established families with large landholdings. There was an informal pecking order based on the length of residence in the village, the amount of land owned, the degree of education, and age. Unlike an industrial society, which places a premium on youth, an agrarian society values the knowledge and judgment based on experience which come with age. Fourth, the mechanism for arriving at collective decisions affecting all of the residents was the village assembly in which all landowning families were represented by the head of the family, usually the father. In these meetings, all interested parties were allowed to present their views, and after interminable talking the leader or leaders would announce a decision based on their reading of the content of the meeting. Decisions were made by consensus rather than by majority vote; by recognizing the existence of minority factions disconcerting cleavages in the community could be revealed. We can see vestiges of this desire to avoid conflict in our own political party conventions when, after a candidate has been chosen on the basis of balloting, a resolution is introduced to nominate the candidate by acclamation.

The abolition of the warrior class in the early years of the Meiji era brought an end to feudalism as a formal system. The warrior groups no longer exist. Still, anti-Establishment critics of leftist persuasion often lament that remnants of feudalism still survive. And they may have a point. Many of the features of Japanese village life described above are still in existence today. In many ways the modern Japanese corporation is a successor to the warrior groups of the Tokugawa period. But before we examine modern corporate structure, it would be well to discuss briefly the structure of groups in Japan today.

The Structure of Groups Today

It may be somewhat misleading to speak of "structure," as groups in Japanese society are typically informal and have no table of organization or set of explicit rules. These groups tend to be small, ranging from one to two dozen members. (When groups grow to be much larger than this subgroups usually develop, splitting off from the main group like multiplying cells.) These small groups form the core groups within large organizations and institutions.

The members of these small groups relate to each other in a hierarchical order. Ranking within the group depends upon several factors: age, the date when the individual was first employed by the firm (in the case of groups within business establishments), and the length of continuous employment in the company. In short, the seniority principle operates. The older persons who have been around for a long time and presumably know more than the youngsters are respected, and the younger newcomers are expected to show deference. In describing this hierarchical structure, Japanese sociologist Chie Nakane gives as an example the university hiking clubs in which members of the junior class carry the heavier loads, put up the tents, and prepare the evening meals under the supervision of the seniors. When the meal is ready, the seniors eat first, served by the juniors.

Since the seniority principle operates, the leader of a group is usually an older person who has attained that position through long service. In a small group in a factory, the leader might be the foreman who has been promoted to that position from the ranks; in an academic situation, the professor who has been on the faculty longest would be the most likely leader.

Of course, the fact that a person has seniority does not necessarily make him a good leader. In the Japanese small group context, the good leader is not the man who is sharp, has done his homework well, and knows all the answers. In fact, a good leader does not concern himself with the details, leaving them to his subordinates. It is more important

that he have the capacity to relate well to his followers, listening to and empathizing with them, showing that he has their welfare at heart, covering up for their shortcomings, and maintaining harmony within the group. In short, he must be a paternalistic leader who looks after his subordinates not only in job-related areas but in personal matters as well. The subordinates, in turn, are obligated to be loyal to the leader, to work hard under his direction, to help him look good by making constructive suggestions, and so on.

Thus, the leader and his followers are bound together by a long-term system of mutual obligation. The relationship is highly personal-ized and embraces virtually all facets of life. Under these circumstances, leadership succession is a difficult problem. When a leader dies or retires the group cannot acquire a new leader from the outside. Outsiders can join a group only by coming in at the bottom and gradually acquiring seniority. Unless the old leader has groomed one of his lieutenants to follow in his footsteps the group may very well disintegrate, in which case the followers will join other groups.

Miss Nakane believes that these types of highly personalized rela-tionships provide the Japanese small group with its driving force. There is much to be said for this interpretation. If a person is not a member of a group he can choose to be lazy, if he wishes. But this is not possible if he joins a group. If he wishes to maintain his good standing within the group he must work hard, for his lack of effort would adversely affect the performance of the group as a whole. Group members will ostracize a persistent slacker, often making him so uncomfortable he will leave the group. The desire to enhance group performance also leads individuals to work overtime, if necessary, to make up for another worker's temporary deficiency caused by illness or other conditions. The hard workers who contribute to the performance of the group win the approval of their fellow members and, of course, the leader.

Decision-making can be a complicated affair within the structure of the small group. A leader, by definition, leads; he tells his subordinates to do this or that, or to refrain from doing something, and presumably he has the authority to make his order stick. The leader of a Japanese small group does not necessarily function in this manner. Let us sup-pose that events or conditions necessitate a change in the way things are done. In this situation, suggestions will emerge from different mem-bers of the group, the pros and cons will be discussed at length, and eventually a large majority will form around one specific proposal. In the end, those who had misgivings will agree to go along with that proposal and a consensus will result.

An able leader will manage to influence the proposal to some extent, but the decision he articulates will be the product of group consensus. This being the case, the leader does not have to sell the decision to his subordinates or persuade them to accept it, as they have already been involved in the decision. When most Japanese speak of "democracy," they have in mind a decision-making process in which there is widespread consultation. When a strong leader or a dominant faction pushes through a measure on the basis of a majority vote, this is often criticized as being "undemocratic."

Small Groups and Industrialization

It should be evident from the foregoing discussion that the structure and function of small groups in Japan is closely related to the character of village life. We see this in the importance attached to personalized relationships, the principle of seniority, the value placed on the welfare of the group as a whole, the process of decision-making by consensus, and the emphasis on conformity. As Japan has industrialized the proportion of the rural population engaged in agriculture has declined, with many workers leaving the villages for the cities. During the period of rapid economic growth in the 1960s, the exodus from the villages was accelerated. But what appears to have happened is that the forms of social organization evolved in the village setting, instead of being cast off completely in the urban environment, have been, to a remarkable degree, incorporated into the industrial structure which emerged. The Japanese have used many features of the traditional culture to facilitate the transition to a new industrial state. We can illustrate this phenomenon by looking at important features of industrial organization in contemporary Japan.

First, let us consider the method by which workers are recruited. Management does not choose employees purely on the basis of ability to perform tasks. According to government surveys, some 30 percent of all employees are hired through some form of personal contact; they are friends, acquaintances, or relatives of people already on the payroll. In addition, companies have established contact with people who run government employment agencies, high school counselors, and others who are in a position to influence prospective workers in the choice of firms, so the proportion of those who get jobs through personal connections of one sort or another is probably higher than the 30 percent reported in surveys.

Management prefers this sort of arrangement because employees hired in this manner are likely to work harder, stay longer, and be more pliant to management wishes than those who secure employment through impersonal means. A worker who has been recruited by a friend or relative, or by his high school teacher, feels a sense of obligation to that person, and will feel it necessary to behave in such a way that he will not embarrass his mentor or cause him to lose face.

Second, the seniority concept developed in village life has been transposed in the industrial structure into the *nenko* system of lifetime employment and wage scales based on length of employment. Contrary to the impression sometimes given in the American press, not all employees have lifetime tenure. It is characteristic of large firms, but not of the smaller enterprises, and does not apply to so-called temporary employees. Perhaps as much as one-third of the entire labor force in the non-agricultural sectors has lifetime tenure. Typically, a young man (the system discriminates against women since most of them presumably want to work only a few years, until they get married) joins a firm after graduation by passing an examination or by being recommended by someone. He is then given specialized training by the company. If he shows promise during the probation period he becomes a permanent employee and stays on until the age of fifty-five, when he retires. Some employees are kept on after the retirement age, but they are considered temporary employees. They are paid less and are not eligible for certain fringe benefits.

Because of labor shortages in recent years, able young men have had opportunities to move on to other firms, and some do so. Quite possibly labor mobility will rise sharply as time goes on, but the number of those who move from one firm to another is likely to remain smaller than in the United States. At present, if an individual does not move before he reaches the age of thirty, he is likely to stay with the firm until he retires. At the age of fifty-five, the employee is entitled to retirement benefits which consist of a lump sum settlement. There are various ways of calculating the amount of this settlement. In one system, the employee receives a sum equal to one month's pay for every year worked, excluding the first four years. The rate of pay used to calculate this settlement is an average of the last four years' wages, which would be higher than wages in his earlier years of employment. The settlement usually is not large enough to afford a reasonably comfortable living for any length of time, especially in view of the rapid rate of inflation which prevails.

In principle, a firm would not fire an employee who had been given lifetime tenure, but there are ways of doing so in cases where economic conditions make it imperative to trim payrolls or employees turn out to be lazy or incompetent. Because of rapid economic growth and the accompanying labor shortage, most companies have not yet been confronted with the problem of having to fire many employees, but a serious economic depression, should one occur, would undoubtedly put the system to a severe test.

A corollary of lifetime employment is the principle of wages based on seniority. Every employee receives a basic wage based upon his educational qualifications. College graduates earn more than high school graduates, who earn more than middle school graduates. Generally, college and high school graduates enter the white-collar ranks, while middle school graduates go into blue-collar jobs. However, with the recent rise in the educational level, more and more high school graduates have been forced to take blue-collar positions.

In addition to the basic wage, employees receive annual increments based partly on work performance, and several other allowances, such as housing and family allowances, all of which favor the older workers. Income rises with seniority, but the rate of increase tends to flatten out as one gets closer to retirement age. The system penalizes younger workers, who are paid less yet are often better trained and more productive than their seniors. If the younger worker stays long enough, his wages will rise, so that over the long haul pay will even out; but young workers who are getting increasingly consumption minded are often restless and do not want to wait. This places a strain on the system, and Japanese managers, with characteristic ingenuity, sometimes meet the problem by giving productive younger workers extra pay in the form of larger allowances without changing the basic wage. It is obvious that the method of paying according to seniority compels employers to exercise care in recruiting workers. They will want to maintain a favorable age mix, because labor costs will rise sharply as workers acquire more seniority.

The system of allowances is one aspect of the paternalism Japanese employers display toward their employees. There are other important forms of paternalism. Practically every Japanese who is regularly employed receives a bonus twice a year, one in mid-summer and the other at the end of the year. The size of the bonus depends on profits, in the case of private industry, and the ability of the unions to bargain with the management. Generally, the bonus is equal to several months' pay, not an insignificant sum. Also, many of the larger companies provide dormitories for unmarried workers and apartments for those with families. This can be an important fringe benefit, because company-owned housing can be obtained at a substantial discount from prevailing market prices. Many firms also seek to meet the recreational needs of their workers. Some own summer resorts where employees and their families can vacation at nominal cost. Companies sometimes co-

operate with labor unions to organize youth sections which arrange outings, dances, sports events, and other forms of recreation for the benefit of their unmarried workers. Paternalism also operates at the upper reaches of corporate life. Top management personnel have access to cars and chauffeurs provided by the company and are given generous expense accounts, which are particularly valuable because such benefits are tax-exempt.

Finally, the structure of the labor unions reflects the influence of traditional values and practices. The basic union is the enterprise union, which is composed of blue-collar and white-collar workers and some lower management personnel of a company or plant. Although craft and industrial unions exist, they are by far in the minority. Enterprise unions are self-contained autonomous units which bargain with management over wages, working conditions, and worker grievances. The union leaders are employees of the firm, and each union collects its own dues, elects officers, and determines policy. Above the enterprise unions are federations at both the prefectural and national levels with which individual unions can affiliate. The majority of unions belong to one of three large national federations. Each year when organized labor launches its "spring offensive" to obtain substantial pay increase, these large national federations coordinate the efforts and set a general pattern for each of the individual enterprise unions to follow. Most of the leaders at the national federation level are strongly committed to Marxist ideology and have marked political leanings. *Sohyo*, the largest federation, which is made up mostly of government workers, supports the Socialist party, while *Domei*, which is dominated by workers in private industry, is closely allied to the more moderate Democratic Socialist party.

The militant leftist orientation of the national federations is not particularly reflected in the policies of the individual enterprise unions. Much of the time, unions and management have been able to achieve some sort of accommodation. This is not so hard to understand in view of the employment practices which have been described above, and in view of the structure of unions and the nature of leadership. Japanese commentators sometimes speak of the dual allegiance of workers. As workers, they want to support their unions, but at the same time they want their company to prosper because they know that they are going to work for the same firm until they retire.

To summarize, the existence of small groups and the nature of employment practices utilized by management has had some positive effects on economic growth. The great advantage small groups have over large groups is that social incentives may be used to promote group goals. Friendship, camaraderie, a sense of belonging, and the approval of one's peers are powerful inducements for individuals to put out maximum effort. By the same token, the threat of withholding these can act as a powerful sanction. By contrast, if one were simply a member of a large organization he would have much less incentive to work hard for the common good, because no matter how hard he worked the contribution he made would seem insignificant in relation to the total output.

Moreover, these social incentives are reinforced by tangible economic rewards. Lifetime employment, a pay scale based on seniority, bonuses, and other fringe benefits tie many workers to their employers. Both employer and employee find themselves in the same boat. Those employed by successful firms with a rising profit curve will prosper. Conversely, those who have hitched their wagons to a firm headed for bankruptcy will suffer and may even be forced to endure much economic insecurity. Obviously, the social system has been a significant factor in Japan's economic progress.

Competition

Although small groups and the spirit of cooperation inherent in them are important, they do not account fully for the dynamic qualities associated with the industrial setup in Japan. Competition, the obverse of cooperation, is also at work. In a sense, the two are antithetical. An exaggerated degree of competition would undercut cooperation, while excessive stress on cooperation would stifle the competitive spirit. Keeping the two in tandem, although difficult, can be highly rewarding.

Let us first consider competition at the individual level. We have noted the strong sense of social hierarchy which prevails in Japan. Despite this, individuals are constantly striving to get ahead. The emergence of the competitive spirit in Japan is not a recent development. Evidence of an earlier emphasis on competition can be found in a classic folktale which is still popular today. This folktale concerns Issun Boshi, a boy who, like Tom Thumb, never grew to normal size. According to the story, one day Issun Boshi told his parents, "I want to go to the capital city and become a great man." His parents gave him their blessing and presented him with a needle, which was to be his sword, and a soup bowl, in which he could float down the river to the city. Arriving safely at his destination, Issun Boshi proceeded to the feudal lord's castle and became the lord's retainer. The lord's daughter, the princess, developed a fondness for him. One day when she went to worship at the local Buddhist temple, Issun Boshi accompanied her as a bodyguard. On the way home, a devil intent on seizing the princess appeared. Coming to her defense, Issun Boshi jumped into the devil's eye and stabbed his eyeball with the needle. The devil fled in great pain, leaving behind a magic wand which would make its owner's wishes come true. The princess picked up the wand and wished that Issun Boshi would grow to be a normal sized boy, whereupon he did. Thus, valor and initiative, aided by a little bit of magic, enabled Issun Boshi to attain his goal.

In the early Meiji period, stress was placed on *risshin shuse*, or "getting on in the world." One of the best selling books of that era was a translation of *Self-Help* by Samuel Smiles, an Englishman who extolled the virtues of hard work and the worldly success it would bring. The book's popularity indicates that it had struck a responsive chord, and many an ambitious schoolboy found inspiration in its message. At that time, getting on in the world implied not only personal success, but also bringing glory to the family and serving the state. Thus, it represented much more than a personal ethic.

Today, as in other societies, there are several roads to fame and fortune in Japan. One way is to acquire an influential patron, in the tradition of Issun Boshi. In the United States as well as in Japan, connections can be helpful, although many people would probably profess a desire to make it on their own. Another way is to exercise entrepreneurial skill. This was the road taken by Kakuei Tanaka, Japan's current prime minister. Tanaka dropped out of school after the ninth grade, migrated to Tokyo, made his fortune as a building contractor, and was elected prime minister by the ruling Liberal Democratic party in the summer of 1972. Robert Cole, an American sociologist who has studied blue-collar workers in two Japanese factories, has reported that he met some workers whose ambition was to become owners of small businesses. These workers knew the risks involved, for the bankruptcy rate among small firms is very high; still they retained the dream of becoming independent businessmen.

For many people, however, the road to getting on in the world passes through the government bureaucracy or the management levels of large corporations. The way toward these goals is clearly marked: progress through the educational system, culminating in admission to the University of Tokyo, the leading government university and training ground of a past, present, and presumably, future elite. Compulsory education extends through junior high school, and those who wish to go beyond that must take competitive entrance examinations at the high school and college levels. In order to get into the University of Tokyo and other top universities, it helps to have attended the better lower schools.

Competition begins virtually at the nursery school level, and there are specialized cram schools where little tots can get coaching that will enable them to impress nursery school teachers and administrators when they go for their entrance examinations. Every ambitious schoolboy can look forward to being subjected to a series of entrance examinations at various levels. It is little wonder that the Japanese describe this process as "examination hell." The closer students get to the university examinations, the harder they must study. Many sit at their desks late into the night under the watchful eyes of their parents, especially the "education mamas," mothers who have high expectations of their children's futures. Those families who can afford it will even hire tutors for their children.

When the fateful examination day arrives, thousands of students, usually accompanied by their mothers, head for the campuses. Universities schedule examinations on different days to enable students to apply at several institutions. This helps the students spread the risk, and no doubt it helps the universities, too, as a substantial examination fee is charged. The results of the examinations are posted in some prominent place and, again, thousands head for the campus to find out whether they have passed or failed. The Japanese are such disciplined people that it is difficult for onlookers watching the faces of the mothers and students who come to check the list to figure out whether they have passed or not. Those who are so unfortunate as to fail all the entrance examinations might well decide to study some more and try again the following year. Such students are known as *ronin*, a term which earlier was applied to samurai in the feudal period who had no feudal lords to serve. Often these students hire tutors to help them, or even attend special schools set up to coach *ronin*. Quite clearly, the present system favors those who have good memories and a great deal of perseverance. It would also appear to work against the unusually creative maverick types who don't fit into the mold. Japanese society must be wasting a certain amount of talent which, if utilized, could stimulate innovation and progress.

Once in college, most students are tired of studying and are not inclined to work hard. Furthermore, it is almost impossible to flunk out of college. The faculty, perhaps in response to their students' lack of enthusiasm, tend to be lackadaisical about their teaching duties; many are frequently late to class or, at times, never show up at all. In large private universities which depend upon tuition for income, classes are huge. A student could conceivably spend four years in class without ever speaking with a professor. It is not surprising, under the circumstances, for some students to become alienated and actively radical.

By the time they are juniors, good students in the leading universities, especially the University of Tokyo, begin to make choices about future careers. One road leads to government service via civil service examinations, while the other leads to the large corporations. When times are good, economics majors at the University of Tokyo may have as many as seven offers. Often they commit themselves to a company by the time they are finishing their junior year. Many students who may have been active in radical causes during their freshman and sophomore years become more conservative when they become upperclassmen to avoid antagonizing prospective employers. No doubt many employers would be reluctant to hire radical activists, but there are some who are not deterred, because they believe radical students to be energetic and aggressive, qualities which companies can use to good advantage. Perhaps such employers also have in mind the Japanese adage, "If one is not a Red by the time he is twenty-five, he is a fool; if he remains a Red after the age of thirty-five, he is a greater fool."

These days, most college students become organization men upon graduation. They become part of the governmental or corporate bureaucratic apparatus. Because of the seniority system, those who enter in any one year tend to go up the ladder together, to a point. There is not room for everyone at the top. Civil servants begin to look for new careers by the time they get to be bureau chiefs. Some run for public office, others move into private organizations. Being human, they will naturally use whatever opportunities present themselves while they are civil servants to pave the way to a second career. For example, an official in the construction ministry might see to it that generous subsidies and contracts go to his home town, thus building up a feeling of goodwill which will be helpful when he becomes a candidate for the House of Representatives from that district in some future election.

Those in middle management positions in large corporations hope that they will be among the few chosen to become top officials in the firm. Those who are so fortunate will not have to retire at fifty-five, but can stay on, earning higher salaries and enjoying larger expense accounts and more generous fringe benefits.

Blue-collar workers cannot look forward to the possibility of reaching the top echelons, but they can and do aspire to upgrade themselves. A machinist in a factory, for instance, can look forward to becoming a foreman or supervisor. According to Robert Cole, "competition becomes stronger as workers approach their late thirties and early forties and aspirations for promotion intensify." (In R. Cole, *The Japanese Blue Collar: The Changing Tradition*, Berkeley: University of California Press, 1971.) He notes, further, that the desire for promotion

strengthens a worker's feelings of loyalty toward the employer and makes him less willing to support militant union demands on the company. Managements are not above utilizing the desire for promotion to intensify competition among workers and increase production. Thus, at both the blue-collar and white-collar levels, the seniority system does not necessarily do away with competition.

Competition in a group-oriented society which stresses social harmony and the spirit of cooperation can be a touchy matter. Competition which is openly aggressive can be counter-productive. There is an old saying, "a protruding stake will be driven into the ground," which derives from a recognition of this fact. When an individual achieves spectacular success, it will likely make his colleagues and friends envious and lead them to make his life uncomfortable and difficult. A blue-collar worker who is overly ambitious and anxious to curry favor in order to enhance his own chances for promotion may find himself ostracized by his fellow workers. Competition, therefore, must be pursued under cover to some extent. A student may actually be studying quite hard, but he must appear to his fellow students to be relaxed about his studies.

Problems associated with competition carried out at the individual level can be lessened if the competition is between or among groups. Those who identify with the group to which they belong can put out extra effort to enhance the group's competitive position without incurring social opprobrium. On the contrary, this effort will bring an individual social praise. Lively competition can exist among families, schools, universities, religious sects, and government agencies. Villages often display a highly competitive spirit. If one of the local notables happens to be running for elective office, the entire population of the village will be under great social pressure to support him. The argument will be made in terms of securing benefits for the group as a whole: if our man is elected, he will use his influence to bring benefits to our village, such as a new schoolhouse, and our neighboring village won't have that advantage.

The most intense sort of competition is probably to be found among the large business firms. Most Japanese place great emphasis on their affiliations. If one asks an American what he does for a living, he will most likely respond that he works with computers, or is an attorney, or an engineer, and so on. If you ask the same question in Japan, the response will be, "I work for Mitsubishi," or "I am employed by Sony." The stress will be on corporate affiliation rather than occupational function. As a member of a corporate group, a Japanese worker can share in its achievements and its reputation. Most Japanese are extremely conscious of relative rankings among corporations, institutions, and universities. They all want to work for a top-ranking company, or attend a top-ranking university. Those who work for a company which is not yet topnotch will strive to improve their firm's ranking. Cutthroat competition exists, and if one company brings out a new product that makes a hit with the public, competitors will quickly jump in to market a similar product.

The highest stratum, above the group and corporation levels, is the nation. Given their long history of isolation and the parochialism it has fostered, the Japanese are highly sensitive to the position of their country in the international hierarchy. Just as they want their family, village, or corporation to be preeminent, they want their nation to be able to attain top rank. A translation of *Robinson Crusoe* published during the Meiji period contained a preface which stated that if the story were read carefully it would show "how by stubborn determination an island can be developed." More recently, the editors of *Forbes* magazine took a look at six giant Japanese trading companies—Mitsubishi, Mitsui, Sumitomo, C. Itoh, Marubeni, and Nissho-Iwai—and discovered that they operated on amazingly thin profit margins, averaging fourteen cents on every $100 of sales. They also learned that these powerful companies were less interested in profits as such than in economic growth and development. A group of C. Itoh executives told a *Forbes* editor that their company's long-range goals were to assure Japan of low-cost raw materials and to help raise the standard of living in Japan. Not one executive said his company was working to make money for their stockholders. (In *Forbes*, May 1, 1972.)

Conflict

The drive for achievement, the force which gives competition its thrust, was present in Japan's past and remains widespread today. The most important institution sustaining this drive is the family. Most parents are ambitious for their children, and want them to be better off in terms of income, social prestige, and economic security than they are. If at least one member of the family achieves fame and fortune, the parents and other children can share in the reflected glory, even if they do not benefit in more practical ways. Parental and family pressures on individuals can be formidable.

On the basis of the Thematic Apperception Test, which involves showing a picture and having subjects tell a story interpreting it, American psychologists have concluded that Japanese families inculcate in their children a commitment to long-range goals and a sensitivity to the opinions and expectations of others. The child works toward these goals not only to satisfy his own ego needs, but also to please his family. Failure to achieve due to lack of effort, rebellion, or criminal behavior results in feelings of guilt. The best way to alleviate these guilt feelings is to mend one's ways and to devote oneself to hard work and success. The way out, then, is repentance. It is interesting to note, in passing, that in Japanese courts a criminal who admits wrongdoing and indicates a determination to reform will impress the judge and most likely be given a light sentence.

The method parents, especially mothers, use to encourage erring children to reform is "silent suffering." In Japanese culture nonverbal forms of communication are highly developed. Anthropologists have noted that Japanese parents tend to guide children by handling and manipulating them rather than by yelling at them, and teachers in traditional arts such as flower arrangement prefer to demonstrate their techniques rather than use detailed verbal instructions. A powerful form of nonverbal communication is illness, especially on the part of the mother. A mother whose son is wayward and is not applying himself may become ill in an unconscious attempt to influence him. The son, realizing that his misbehavior drove his mother to illness, will vow to exert himself in atonement.

In most cultures, the transition to adulthood is accompanied by a certain amount of tension, but in Japan, given the family pressure that can be generated, the amount of tension can be unbearably high. Indirect evidence of this may be found in national suicide rates. In most countries, suicide rates rise according to age. The rate is higher among older people than among the young. An unusual feature of the suicide rate in Japan is that there is an upward bulge among those in their upper teens and twenties. This is the time when young people, especially males, are subjected to the examination hell and to possible conflict with the family over marriage partners. A young man may fall in love with a girl whom he has met in college or in the office, but the family may not approve and would prefer that he follow the more traditional form of arranged marriage. Unable to resolve the conflict between loyalty to his family and fulfillment of personal wishes, he may choose suicide as a way out. The Japanese have a special term, *shinju*, or "lovers' suicide," for the case of a boy and girl who are unable to marry because of parental objections and decide to commit suicide together. A classic method is for the lovers to jump into an active volcano.

In addition to family pressures, most individuals find that their involvement in group life often constrains their freedom to behave in ways which are personally most congenial to them. To maintain effective group relationships, most people must pay the price of accommodating themselves to group norms and goals. In extreme cases, the price can be high.

The most celebrated play in the Kabuki repertoire is the story of the forty-seven *ronin* or masterless samurai. A drama based on an incident which took place in the early eighteenth century, it is still tremendously popular among Kabuki buffs. In the tale, the feudal lord is forced to disembowel himself (one of the methods by which a samurai can die with honor). His crime was to pull his sword and attack another feudal lord who was visiting him. The visitor had repeatedly insulted him, presumably because he was not being bribed sufficiently. Seeing that grave injustice had been done to their master, the samurai, led by one of their number, Oishi, vowed to avenge the death of their lord. The offender, knowing that the forty-seven *ronin* might be after him, was constantly on his guard. So the *ronin* scattered and Oishi, hoping to lull his adversary into a state of complacency, abandoned his wife and children and took to drinking openly and leading a dissolute life. Eventually, Oishi's behavior convinced the feudal lord that he was no longer in danger, and he relaxed his defenses. In the Kabuki play, the denouement takes place on a brilliant revolving stage complete with falling snow. With Oishi in the lead, the band of samurai overcome the lord's bodyguard and finally avenge their master. In reality, the samurai were condemned to death for their deed, but the court allowed them to retain their honor by disemboweling themselves. They became national heroes and were buried together in a graveyard which to this day attracts numerous visitors.

A more recent example of the sacrifices conformity to group norms entails involved a Japanese soldier, Shoichi Yokoi, a tailor's apprentice who had been drafted into the army during World War II and sent to Guam. During the American invasion of the island in 1944, he and others fled into the jungle to avoid capture. There he hid for twenty-eight years. He was accidentally discovered in 1972 and, although the war had ended long before, he refused to surrender because the Japanese army had instructed him never to surrender to the enemy. His case created a sensation in Japan, and was widely reported by the world press. After he was flown back to Japan, he was shown the gravestone which his family had erected for him. He had returned from the dead, but he found that readjustment to modern Japanese life was more than he could handle, and for a time he was confined to an institution. According to recent reports, he subsequently married, which suggests that he recovered. In any case, fidelity to group norms can indeed exact a high toll.

The Problem of Individuation

Not surprisingly, youth are sometimes moved to rebel against parental and group pressures. Robert J. Lifton, an American psychiatrist who undertook in-depth interviews with a sample of Japanese youth, found that they were much concerned with the idea of selfhood (*shutaisei*), or living by one's own personal convictions and having a social commitment to work with like-minded people to achieve historical goals. The conscious ideal of many young Japanese is to be progressive, new, innovative, active, independent, logical, realistic, tough-minded, and scientific—a syndrome which might be termed "active-Western-masculine." What they wish to avoid is becoming unprogressive, passive, dependent, irrational, tradition-minded, and unscientific—in short, "passive-Japanese-feminine." Yet Japanese youth cannot succeed in avoiding completely what they profess to dislike. To renounce Japanese culture in total would be tantamount to cutting themselves off from their cultural heritage. So they are forced to compromise. Because Japanese culture remains group-oriented, despite modernization and Western influences, the young are forced to seek "self-expression via the group," Lifton notes. Thus student rebels and revolutionaries join the radical *Zengakuren* (National Federation of Student Self-Government Associations), and from time to time take to the streets to do battle with the police. In recent years, the *Zengakuren* has become fragmented, with small splinter groups breaking away and regrouping. Today, although most student organizations claim to be the heirs of the Marxist tradition, they actually occupy a broad political spectrum. Some are controlled by the Japanese Communist party, but others consider the party to be too conservative and take a more nihilistic stance. They wish to destroy the existing society, but have no idea what should take its place.

One should not get the impression that all Japanese youth are radical activists bent on destroying the Establishment. As is true in other countries, the activists represent a small minority of the students. Most young people ultimately find a niche in society. One of the consequences of the rapid economic growth of the 1960s has been a decline in politicization among the youth. Every year, thousands of young men and women move to the industrial cities from the rural areas. Had they remained in the villages, these young people would have become enmeshed in the social networks which blanket the rural communities and, through these networks, would have been mobilized to vote and take part in local political activities. Having escaped to the anonymous big city and become increasingly mobile, they have not yet developed local ties and connections, and many of them do not even bother to vote. Certainly politics is not one of their main concerns in life. Rather, their thoughts are mostly on acquiring enough money to buy the good things in life—fashionable clothes, television sets, automobiles, and other consumer goods—a desire for which is stimulated by the constant bombardment of consumer advertising in the mass media. Japan, like other nations, has reached the stage of mass society.

Safety Valves

We have already touched upon some of the conflictual situations inherent in Japanese society and culture—cooperation vs. competition, parents vs. children, and individuals vs. groups. No society is perfect, and perhaps this is to the good, for change and progress come about when people are dissatisfied. Dissatisfaction gives rise to social tensions, and attempts to reduce tension lead to improved conditions. Personal and social tensions can have positive effects, but in excessive amounts it can be destructive. Every society needs safety valves which will prevent an explosion from occurring. Like other peoples, the Japanese have their methods of release.

Foreign tourists often remark upon the large number of small bars which dot large cities like Tokyo. If one walks through the back alleys, one is confronted by a panorama of neon signs advertising bars with exotic names. Almost all of these establishments have hostesses to make the customers feel relaxed and welcome. The businessman who has had an especially difficult day can tell his troubles to a sympathetic hostess who will sit with him at a table. A group of white-collar workers might stop off at a bar on the way home from the office. In the relaxed atmosphere created by a few drinks, they might give their supervisor an earful of their gripes about office routine, something they wanted to get off their chests but were unable to say in the office. The total daily take of the thousands of bars in Tokyo alone must come to an incredible sum, and one would have to presume that those who paid these sums felt they were getting their money's worth. Those bars evidently satisfy a need in the society.

Some observers have suggested that participation in political demonstrations by unionized workers also serves to let off steam. Workers find it difficult to openly oppose management, for reasons we have already touched upon: company paternalism, lifetime tenure, enterprise unionism, and the tendency of unions to identify with firms. Yet there are real differences of interest between management and labor in the areas of production quotas, working conditions, and, above all, wage levels.

It is the responsibility of union leaders to get as much as they can for the workers, and in order to stand up to management in defense of worker rights they need what Robert Cole calls the "moral armor" provided by Marxist ideology. Without it, union leaders might not be able to mount and sustain opposition to management. For the rank-and-file members, union leaders and radical slogans have great symbolic value. They symbolize willingness to oppose management. But this does not mean that workers have accepted Marxist ideology and the implications of the notion of class conflict. Thus, when workers respond to the call of the giant labor federations and their own enterprise union leaders to participate in political demonstrations, they are often acting out in the streets the opposition to management they cannot easily express on the job.

In this sense, political demonstrations may serve as a catharsis, enabling a more harmonious relationship to exist between management and labor. It is worth noting that many of the large-scale demonstrations which have occurred in recent years have involved outside targets, such as the United States-Japan Mutual Security Treaty, American bases in Japan, the visit of American nuclear aircraft carriers, or the proposed visit of the prime minister to some foreign country. One seldom hears of large-scale demonstrations directed at domestic targets, such as the giant companies which dominate the economy.

Participation in political demonstrations and frequenting bars, which we have defined as safety valves which ameliorate personal and social tensions, involve interaction with others. There is another important safety valve which does not involve others, and that is communion with nature, natural objects, and natural beauty. Few peoples in the world have been able to achieve the sort of closeness to rocks, flowers, trees, water, mountains, and fish that the Japanese manifest in their daily lives. Unlike the basic attitude of Western man, who sees God, and man made in His image, at the center of the universe, the Japanese perceive man as one of the vast array of objects and forces in nature. The Japanese regulate their lives to conform with nature. They are profoundly aware of the comings and goings of the seasons; the food they prepare, the clothing they wear, and the color and design of the bedding they use, all reflect the seasons. Moreover, colorful flowers, bamboo leaves, autumn leaves, and other natural objects form the basis of designs in Japanese clothing and household furnishings. In the house, flowers are arranged in beautiful containers and dwarfed trees may be placed on the veranda.

The contemplation and enjoyment of natural beauty and works of art representing nature are intended to be highly individualistic. Pictures and other artistic objects are not displayed in profusion; rather, they are kept in a storeroom and brought out one at a time, according to appropriateness to the season or occasion. Fosco Maraini, a perceptive observer of Japanese culture, has noted, quite correctly, that museums and art galleries are alien to the Japanese mentality. The Japanese now have these institutions, but they have been imported from Western culture.

We can get some idea of the high value placed on nature in Japan from a poem written by Ryokan, a thirteenth-century Buddhist priest, on his deathbed. Obviously a man of great compassion, he had built charity hospitals and is reputed to have carried a leper on his back to the city and helped him beg for alms. But instead of looking back on these achievements, he wrote,

> *For a memento of my existence*
> *What shall I leave (I need not leave anything)?*
> *Flowers in the spring, cuckoos in the summer,*
> *and the maple leaves*
> *in the autumn.*

It is not surprising, given this sensitivity to nature, that the Japanese excel in aesthetics. There are few people in the world who have a more acute sense of beauty, proportion, and texture than the Japanese. A clue to the predominant role aesthetic matters play in Japanese culture may be found in the language. Compared to English, Japanese contains many more terms to express different kinds of beauty, and some of them, like *shibui* (literally, "astringent," referring to an avoidance of ostentation), while not yet found in English dictionaries, have been adopted in America by designers and interior decorators.

A memorable example of *shibui* is the famous garden in the Ryoanji, a Zen Buddhist temple built in about 1500. It is a garden, but it has no plants or flowers, only greenish lichens and moss. The garden consists of about a dozen stones and rocks, grouped spatially in a random manner, much as one finds rocks in a natural setting. The remainder of the garden consists of white sand raked in parallel lines suggesting a flowing stream of water. It is so simple, and yet so beautiful, that those who come to see the garden stand in awe and silence. It says everything, and there is no need to embellish it with words.

CHAPTER THREE

TOWARD AFFLUENCE

IN 1945 JAPAN'S ECONOMIC future looked bleak indeed. The war, which had begun with an invasion of North China in 1937, had escalated into a major conflict with the Great Powers. Ultimately the war effort depleted stockpiles of vital materials needed to carry on the fighting. Oil became so scarce that even gasoline needed to train fighter pilots could no longer be spared. By 1944, the American capture of important air bases in the South Pacific brought the islands within bomber range. As a result, Tokyo and several other metropolitan centers were leveled, and virtually every city suffered damage from fire bombs unleashed by American airplanes. The climax of the air attack came in 1945 when the cities of Hiroshima and Nagasaki were obliterated by atom bombs. Although some military leaders sought to prolong the war and even talked of defending the islands against an expected American invasion by mobilizing the population to fight with bamboo spears, saner minds prevailed. An exhausted Japan chose to surrender and accept military occupation for the first time in her history.

After surrender, the Japanese were confined to the four main islands; the colonial possessions, along with the vast amount of capital which had been invested in Korea, Formosa, Manchuria, and other areas, had disappeared. Similarly, the extensive network of offices and trade connections which Mitsui, Mitsubishi, and other large international trading firms had established throughout the world to promote foreign trade no longer existed. The traditional markets and sources of raw materials were gone. Within the country, the rationing system broke down with the end of hostilities, forcing urban dwellers to make forays into the countryside in search of food. They gave those valuables which had survived the bombing raids—clothing, jewels, household equipment—to farmers in trade for rice and vegetables. Those who managed to survive by resorting to such tactics were soon assailed on another front by runaway inflation. Prices had been rising throughout the war, but the rise accelerated sharply after surrender.

During the 1930s, one dollar could buy a little more than four yen; by the time the inflation stabilized in the late 1940s, one dollar was worth 360 yen, and it remained at that level until the recent revaluation, which has so far made the yen a little less than 20 percent more valuable in comparison to the American dollar.

In short, the depletion of material resources, the destruction of cities, including industrial plants, the loss of markets, and economic dislocation added up to a bleak picture. No observer, foreign or Japanese, predicted that within twenty years Japan would become one of the world's leading economic powers.

The Human Factor

There is no comprehensive explanation for this almost miraculous recovery from the ruins of war and defeat. About all one can do is list several factors which logic tells us must have contributed to it. Among the most important of these would be the human factor. Although the bombings destroyed numerous factories, they did not wipe out the fund of scientific knowledge and technological skills which had been accumulated over the recent decades. As we have seen, mass education had taken hold, giving rise to a literate and relatively well-educated population. Thus, those who had not previously acquired training in useful industrial skills possessed sufficient general background to be trainable in short order.

In addition, the strong group orientation and the fiercely competitive spirit described in the previous chapter not only survived the vicissitudes of war and defeat, but may in fact have been strengthened by the turmoil. In short, given leadership and the right environment, the human materials for an economic revival were present.

The Environment

Let us first look at the international environment. On the international front, with the ending of the war and the coming of political independence to many Asian and African countries, world attention was turned to the formidable problems of reconstruction. The destruction caused by the war, combined with the slowdown in maintenance of all kinds of equipment and facilities as a result of the economic depression of the 1930s, produced a tremendous pent-up demand for goods and services throughout the world. If the Japanese produced goods of adequate quality which were competitively priced, there was bound to be a market for them.

The policies of the American-dominated military occupation (here considered to be part of the international rather than the domestic environment) also contributed to Japan's revival. The occupation involved a social engineering project intended to transform Japanese culture and institutions in a fundamental way. In the beginning, the dominant theme of the occupation was reform: reapportioning the land, breaking up the industrial monopolies, democratizing the political structure, and so on. The thrust of these reforms was to redistribute both wealth and political power. Briefly stated, the many profited at the expense of the few. Moreover, the occupation policies had the effect of loosening up the social, economic, and political systems. The resultant fluidity enabled ambitious, innovative persons to get ahead. It has been reported that the founder of Honda Motorcycle Company started with a few hundred dollars in capital. Matsushita Electric Company, now listed on the New York Stock Exchange, is another example of a successful firm started by an enterprising entrepreneur in the postwar period.

Within a few years the occupation policy shifted from reform to recovery. The onset of the cold war, together with the American realization that a poverty-stricken Japan would require continued aid, led policy makers in Washington to work for Japan's economic revival. An economically strong Japan militarily allied with the United States came to be regarded as a bulwark against the further spread of Communism in Asia. By the time the occupation came to an end with the peace treaty signed in San Francisco in 1951, considerable recovery had taken place, thanks to American aid (which the Japanese later repaid at the rate of twenty-five cents on the dollar) and Japan's reentry into the world market.

Still, at the time independence was restored, the country had not been able to return to the prewar levels of production and consumption. Japan was still relatively poor and her military strength was virtually nonexistent. Furthermore, by 1951 a Communist regime had been established in China, and the Korean war had taken place on Japan's doorstep. Unaided, the Japanese would have had difficulty defending themselves against an external attack. Realizing this, General Mac-

Arthur had authorized the establishment of a small military force in 1950. Nevertheless, persistent pacifist sentiment in the country, and the clause in the American-written Constitution of 1946 which banned rearmament, prevented the creation of a large military establishment.

Thus, at the signing of the peace treaty in San Francisco, a separate military agreement was entered into, with the United States assuming the obligation to defend Japan. Although the military treaty was later modified, the United States is to this day obligated to defend Japan, and to that end maintains naval and air bases in Japan and Okinawa. The military alliance with the United States has continued to irritate many people, especially those on the Left; yet at the same time, the alliance has permitted Japan to avoid a heavy national defense burden. In contrast to many countries which spend anywhere from 5 to more than 10 percent of the Gross National Product for defense, Japan has consistently spent about 1 percent, or even less. This has meant that resources not utilized for defense purposes could be channeled into more productive uses.

Let us now turn to the domestic environment. A remarkable feature on the domestic scene is the essential continuity of leadership. Unquestionably, war, defeat, and occupation brought a host of changes, but that they were not revolutionary is demonstrated by the composition of persons in top positions. To be sure, the occupation did conduct a purge of leaders, but this primarily affected professional military personnel. A few bureaucrats were removed, but most of them were allowed to stay on, simply because the occupation authorities decided to work through the existing governmental machinery rather than to set up an alternative military government. Under the circumstances, the elimination of thousands of civil servants would have been counterproductive.

Political leadership also included many carry-overs from the prewar period. As soon as the war ended, old-line party politicians reemerged to organize new parties with names more appropriate to the times, such as Progressive and Liberal. Despite the nomenclature, these were conservative parties dedicated to promoting traditional values and maintaining the capitalist system. In 1955 the two major conservative parties, Liberal and Democratic, merged to form the Liberal Democratic party, which continues to govern to this day. Actually, except for a brief interlude when a coalition which contained a Socialist party came to power, the conservatives have been in control since 1945. Hence, unlike many of the Third World countries which have been plagued by political insecurity, Japan has enjoyed a stable political system run by a group of political leaders who favor business interests.

東南雲金剛　意生金剛

種子

黒色

As for business leadership, for a brief period the occupation engaged in trust-busting activities. Shortly after the war the large industrial combines (*zaibatsu*) were dissolved in an effort to promote economic democracy. The dissolution order, however, only affected the top holding companies. The various families who owned shares in these holding companies were compelled to turn over the stock to a government agency in return for government bonds. Family control over the large combines was broken. In this sense, it is fair to say that the prewar *zaibatsu* no longer exists. Today, ownership of corporate enterprise is fairly widely distributed. There is much activity on the Tokyo Stock Exchange, and millions of individuals buy and sell stocks. Roughly one in five Japanese owns securities. However, in many corporations, especially the older ones, the principal stockholders tend to be financial institutions like banks. In any case, regardless of who owns the stock, corporations are largely run by professional managers who are there because they have management skills which are needed.

Japan's bureaucratic, political, and business leaders are able to work together in a remarkably harmonious way. For one thing, many individual elite members have strong family and school ties which serve to bind them into a cohesive group. Children of prominent business executives sometimes marry children of politicians and prominent bureaucrats. A great majority of the ruling elite, moreover, are graduates of the University of Tokyo; many of them have been classmates, or have studied under the same professors. A powerful tie which binds the business community to politicians is, of course, that bane of all contemporary politics, money. Politicians cannot function, especially during national elections, without large sums of money. Political leaders, therefore, regularly turn to the large corporations for funds. Political contributions are channeled both to the Liberal Democratic party headquarters and to individual leaders, who then distribute the funds to their followers.

The bureaucrats come into the picture through their political activities after retirement from government service. Civil servants retire young, certainly not later than fifty-five. Aided by the endorsement of the Liberal Democratic party, those who have political ambitions run for elective office, hoping to represent their home towns in the House of Representatives or the House of Councillors. Since many voters are favorably impressed by candidates whose credentials include government service, they are often elected.

Once in office they rise rapidly to positions of influence within the Liberal Democratic party. Their expertise and experience in administration, as well as their connections with administrators in the government agencies, give them powerful leverage within the party. Other bureaucrats who do not choose to enter politics have no difficulty finding employment in corporations or in organizations such as pressure groups. In these instances, employers are particularly interested in contacts such men have in the government. These interrelationships have resulted in a domestic environment which is highly favorable to businessmen and business activity.

The Role of Government

As was suggested in Chapter One, the beginnings of industrialization in Japan owed much to government initiative. During the latter part of the nineteenth century the government provided subsidies, set up model factories, and sold government-owned industries to private interests. Since that time the government has continued to be involved, sometimes indirectly, in industrial development. The Japanese National Railways, a government corporation, owns and operates the main land transportation system, and the government is the principal stockholder in Japan Air Lines. The postal and telegraph system is also run by the government, and salt and tobacco are government monopolies.

Where it is not directly involved, the government steps in from time to time to lend a hand. For example, in 1964 and 1965 the economy suffered a recession, which resulted in a bear market on the Tokyo Stock Exchange. To prevent a further decline in stock prices the government combined with industry to form a corporation which bought shares to shore up the market. Some years later, after the market recovered, the stock holdings were sold off and the corporation was dissolved. It is hard to imagine the American government taking this sort of action.

Although several government agencies are concerned with the state of the economy, the most important ministry of economic affairs is the Ministry of International Trade and Industry (abbreviated as MITI). MITI is particularly preoccupied with the competitive position of Japan in world trade, and works constantly to protect and promote Japanese business abroad. Despite occupation-sponsored antitrust laws which are still on the books, the Ministry has forced mergers of smaller firms in order to create companies with sufficient capital to compete effectively with American and European corporations. A case in point is a series of mergers in the automobile industry. At one time there were nine small firms, but at present the industry is dominated by the makers of Toyota and Datsun.

MITI also takes a protectionist stance toward the importation of foreign goods and capital. Despite pressure from the United States and European countries to liberalize trade and investment, a number of items are still subject to high tariffs. In many lines of business foreign capital is allowed to be invested only in the form of joint enterprises with Japanese firms, and the amount of stock owned by foreigners must be less than 50 percent. The Japanese government, however, is taking steps to remove these restraints as the economy becomes stronger and better able to weather foreign competition. An American, for instance, can now have 100 percent ownership of a Japanese-style inn.

Government actions can also have far-reaching effects in the area of tax policies. Those who have studied Japan's tax structure have come to the conclusion that it is geared toward accumulation of capital, thus encouraging rapid economic growth. For instance, no income tax is levied on capital gains earned through trading in stocks. Moreover, income from interest and dividends is not taxed as ordinary income but is subject to special rates, which go up and down from time to time but are still quite low (from 10 to 15 percent). These measures encourage savings and investments, and tend to favor those who have money. To that extent, Japan's tax system is regressive rather than progressive. Both personal and corporate income taxes have been lowered occasionally, resulting in the lessening of the tax burden in terms of real income. The government is also generous about taxing expense accounts. In general, the tax structure would appear to be favorable to business enterprise.

In keeping with its involvement in the economy, the government engages in economic planning. The Economic Planning Agency, which has a large staff of professional economists, is responsible for detailed projections and plans. Perhaps the most widely publicized example of economic planning is the income-doubling plan announced in 1961 during the prime ministership of the late Hayato Ikeda.

Ikeda, a former bureaucrat and tax expert, became prime minister in 1960, shortly after the large-scale demonstrations which followed the ratification of the mutual security treaty with the United States. In order to defuse the political situation, he adopted the program of doubling Japanese national income within a decade, on the theory, one would suppose, that no one could be opposed to prosperity.

The plan itself was the product of the Economic Planning Agency, which has close relations with MITI because many of its personnel had originally worked for MITI. The Ministry of Finance, which urged liberalization of trade and control over foreign exchange, opposed the plan. The more protectionist MITI favored strengthening the economy through rapid growth and structural change before liberalizing trade.

To achieve a doubling of national income in a period of ten years would have required an average annual growth of a little more than 7 percent, and many economists were skeptical that this could be done, but it was. In fact, an average rate of real growth of more than 10 percent was maintained throughout the 1960s.

High Growth in the 1960s

Such a consistently high growth rate was unparalleled in the world; most of the industrialized countries, including the United States, averaged between 4 and 6 percent real growth per year. To help explain what occurred during the 1960s in Japan, we can cite at least four factors in addition to the positive role of the government already discussed above: (1) the transformation of a semi-developed economy into a mature one; (2) technological borrowing from abroad; (3) large-scale private investment in productive facilities; and (4) the availability of raw materials.

Economic analysts have often used the term "dual economy" to characterize the Japanese situation. There is a highly visible modern sector—steel and electronics are good examples—which relies heavily upon computers, automation, and up-to-date production facilities. But side by side with the modern, and to some extent supporting it, is a more traditional sector which relies on more primitive methods of production and suffers from under-capitalization. Agriculture is one part of this traditional sector.

Unlike Great Britain, which made the decision to downgrade agriculture early in the industrialization process, Japan stressed farming until recently. Before the war, as part of its defense program, the military promoted agriculture in order to assure a steady supply of food from domestic sources. The military also prized farmers because they were looked upon as a repository of traditional values and virtues, and because peasant sons made good draftees. In recent years the defense problem has become less important. Since the war the farmers have consistently supported the Liberal Democratic party at the polls, and politicians have reciprocated by supporting agriculture through a price support program. As late as 1960, one out of every three persons in the work force was engaged in the primary industries of agriculture, fishing, and forestry.

Unlike agriculture in America, which relies on large commercial enterprises, farming in Japan is on a miniscule scale. The average farm comprises several acres, and is operated mostly with family labor using hand implements and small, gasoline-powered equipment. Perhaps it would be more accurate to call this gardening rather than farming. Despite the smallness of scale, Japanese farmers are highly productive. Collectively, they have been able to supply as much as 80 percent of the food consumed in the country. Still, because of the small size of the average farm, farmers have not been in a position to derive the economic benefits inherent in large-scale production. They are able to make a living wage, but not much more.

When the economic expansion of the 1960s occurred, large numbers of young men and women who were born and raised on farms moved to the towns and cities, lured by the bright lights and the prospect of employment in industry. In 1964 they numbered about 890,000. Since then there has been a slight decline in this urban influx, with the 1969 figure standing at 796,000. Of course, not all of them stay in the cities. Some find the smog, noise, and overcrowding more than they bargained for, and approximately one in four returns to the rural areas in what the Japanese call the "U-turn."

Many older farmers have also decided to take industrial employment. Every year during the slack season, thousands migrate to the cities in search of temporary jobs and return to their homes in time for spring planting. Other farmers become commuters. Because of high land costs, new factories are constantly being established some distance from the cities, and thanks to a very efficient system of public transportation, farmers can take factory employment, leaving the farm chores to their wives and children and the grandparents. Consequently, in recent years the number of farmers who depend wholly on farming for their livelihood has declined steadily. Full-time farmers, by the way, are buying up more land and specializing in commercial crops such as fruits. By 1970 about one-half of the farm families obtained the major part of their income from non-farming sources. According to the most recent figures, which are for 1971, the work force in primary industries has been reduced to 16 percent, one-half of its 1960 size. Put in another way, the farm areas have provided a substantial part of the additional labor force which made the economic expansion possible.

Another portion of the so-called traditional sector is composed of the small and medium-sized industries. Small enterprises employing a few workers are more prominent in Japan than in any industrialized country in Europe. In 1969 roughly one-half of all establishments engaged in manufacturing, and almost 80 percent of those engaged in wholesale and retail trade, employed only from one to four persons.

On the outskirts of the downtown area of Tokyo a large number of small shops cluster around bus and streetcar stops. Every residential area has a small shopping section consisting typically of one or two

butcher shops, vegetable stands, bookstores, tea stores, hardware stores, and so on. In the back alleys there are also numerous small shops where workmen make parts for bicycles, vacuum cleaners, and other appliances.

There are several reasons for the prevalence of these smaller businesses. For one thing, the long historical process of modernization did not greatly affect Japanese life styles until fairly recently. Although Japanese branches of McDonald's hamburgers and Kentucky Fried Chicken attract hordes of customers in the metropolitan areas, the Japanese still eat the more traditional fish, bean curd, pickles, and rice. In the same way, although Western-style suits and dresses are worn extensively, the Japanese have not completely discarded the traditional kimono. The same thing is true of household furnishings.

As long as the traditional items are in demand, they can be supplied by manufacturers and vendors operating on a small scale. However, the long-term trend is clearly against the small businessman. Although the day when the housewife does all of her grocery shopping in a large supermarket has not yet arrived, the small family-operated retail store with a few hundred dollars' worth of goods on the shelves will eventually disappear.

Another reason for the persistence of small-scale business establishments has to do with the very structure of the economy. Giant firms like Toyota Motors, which are well known in the United States, actually top pyramids of smaller companies. In return for financial investments, the smaller businesses supply the parent firm with parts. The subcontractors, in turn, maintain satellite firms, making the base of the pyramid quite extensive. In some cases the top firm encourages a trusted long-time employee to go into business manufacturing components for sale to the parent company. The firm may even provide part of the capital and sell obsolete machinery to the employee at attractive prices in order to enable him to get started. If the subcontractor prospers, he may branch out into other lines. To facilitate this, he may follow the same pattern, setting up some other individual as his subcontractor by lending him capital and providing other forms of assistance.

As long as the company at the top of the pyramid is able to purchase and use its share of the total output of the lesser firms, they will all prosper. However, if a recession forces the top firm to cut back on its orders, the subcontractors will be severely affected. This is one reason the bankruptcy rate among small firms is so high, especially during periods of economic contraction. By the same token, this arrangement has advantages for the large firm at the top. For one thing, large firms can make their capital stretch because the subcontractors also have to put up a large share of the capital. This also helps large firms avoid the problem of being stuck with a large labor force which cannot be reduced quickly in size because of the lifetime employment system. This arrangement gives large companies much more flexibility.

One of the difficulties many of the smaller firms have faced, particularly since the growth rate began to accelerate in 1965, is a shortage of labor. Since the larger, nationally known companies pay better wages, give more generous fringe benefits, and are more prestigious, young workers generally prefer to work for them. The proportion of younger workers in small establishments has declined in recent years, while the percentage of older employees has risen. During the 1960s, there was a gradual shift of younger workers from the less productive sectors of the economy, namely agriculture and small industries, to the more productive, highly capitalized, large industrial establishments. This shift has affected the productivity figures; during the 1960s, labor productivity in Japan rose a little more than 280 percent, in contrast to the United States, where it rose about 150 percent.

The second factor which contributed to the high growth rate of the 1960s is large-scale technological borrowing from abroad. Relatively speaking, Japanese business does not spend large sums for research and development. Rather, they have made a practice of licensing patents and industrial processes on a royalty basis from the more advanced industrial countries. When a corporation secures a license to use a patent, it may then call in its engineering staff to find ways to improve the product. The importation of technology, especially in chemical and heavy industries and related fields, has increased over the years. In 1961, 122 licenses were purchased; by 1968 the figure had risen to 1,061, representing an eightfold increase. Royalty payments have also increased, reaching almost $300 million in 1968. It should be noted that the Japanese have also licensed their own products and processes to foreign countries, but on a much smaller scale.

The third factor, large-scale private investment in productive facilities, is basic to growth. In Chapter Two we touched on the spirit of competition which permeates the business world in Japan. During the 1960s, every company sought to expand production and capture a larger share of the market. This drive may be attributed in part to pride. Each firm wanted to be number one in the rankings. But there was also a practical consideration here. When many firms compete to add capacity in the hope of capturing a larger share of the market, soon there will be excess capacity, leading to a downward trend in prices and profits. Typically, at that point the government will intervene and compel manufacturers to cut back on production in order to stabilize prices.

Since the amount of the cutback will be based on a percentage of rated productive capacity, those who have invested heavily in additional capacity will be rewarded by a larger share of the market, while those who have not invested heavily will be penalized. We can get some idea of the increase in investment in productive facilities by looking at some statistics relating to the top 1,200 to 1,300 firms in Japan. In 1960, these firms invested a total of nearly $3.5 billion; this figure rose to nearly $4.4 billion in 1965, and by 1970 it had risen to approximately $13 billion. The same trend can be seen in production figures. Crude steel production, for instance, rose from roughly twenty-eight million tons in 1961 to more than eighty-two million tons in 1969.

The capital to build these new production facilities came mostly from domestic sources, since the Japanese have been reluctant to allow foreign capital to come into the country on a large scale. On the average, a little more than one-half of the capital investment mentioned above came from funds generated within the companies; that is, retained profits and depreciation charges. In addition, during the early 1960s corporations sold additional stock as well as some debentures, and invested the proceeds. In the latter half of the decade, however, not much stock was sold.

Short-term loans, mostly from banks, are also an important source of investment capital. When these short-term loans become due, new loans are obtained to repay them. In American corporations, the proportion of the total capitalization represented by shares of stock, or equity, is quite large. Even in the case of utilities, which because of the nature of their business must borrow substantial sums, the ratio of equity to debt is usually around 50 percent, if not better. Even American Telephone and Telegraph, whose financial soundness no one doubts, prefers not to get its indebtedness too high for fear its credit rating will fall.

Those who are accustomed to American business standards would be horrified if they were to examine the balance sheets of some of the leading Japanese corporations. Japanese companies generally operate with huge amounts of borrowed money. In some cases equity may be as low as 20 percent of the total capitalization, or even less. By American standards, many Japanese firms are practically bankrupt. Yet they not only manage to function, they grow and prosper. Incidentally, the low equity ratio is one reason many Japanese corporations are reluctant to allow American and other foreign firms to buy an interest in their business. If, for instance, the Japanese equity were only 20 percent and an American company sought to buy 35 percent ownership, the foreign corporation could gain control.

The banks are able to supply large amounts of capital to corporations because there is a steady flow of savings by millions of individuals. The Japanese are addicted to saving. Between 1955 and 1965, for instance, an average of 25 percent of the net total national product was saved. Individuals save as much as 12 percent of their income. Surveys by Japanese government agencies show that many working class families like to have an amount equal to one year's income put away in a bank or postal savings account.

There are a number of reasons for this sort of behavior. In general, the Japanese are a future-oriented people; tomorrow, next week, next year, and next decade are more important to them than today. They tend to plan toward the time when their children will be going to college, and toward retirement and old age. This is important, because the country has not yet worked out an adequate system of old-age security through governmental programs.

The salary system would also appear to work in favor of saving. Most wage earners receive bonuses amounting to several months' pay twice a year. In a great many instances, household budgets adjust themselves to the monthly income. Most people discover that as their monthly pay check goes up, their expenditures tend to keep pace. Since a bonus is paid only twice a year, it does not enter into the monthly budget. So when a worker gets his summer bonus, the family may decide to use some of it to buy the television set they have been wanting, but certainly a portion will be saved. Without this propensity to save on the part of millions of people, Japanese banks would not have been able to finance the corporate expansion of the 1960s.

Japanese banks have another role which deserves some comment. Bankers are generally conservative people who discipline themselves to stick to safe investments. Since they are dealing with other people's money, they are concerned with the preservation of capital. Foreign bankers could well conclude that Japanese banks are willing to make loans involving a higher degree of risk than would be considered prudent in many other countries. On the face of it, loans involving high risk are no doubt made, but the Japanese banking system is unusual. There are several groups of large banks and firms which are closely intertwined.

For instance, in 1968 twenty-five firms were closely associated with the Mitsui Bank, obtaining anywhere from 15 to 70 percent of their financing from this one bank. Among these firms, in addition to several Mitsui companies engaged in mining and shipbuilding, were such well-known corporations as Sony, Toyota Motors, and Toshiba. There are a number of other such groups organized around leading banks: Mitsubishi, Sumitomo, Fuji, Sanwa, and Yasuda, to name a few. One advantage afforded by this sort of group structure is that it makes it possible to spread the risk to some extent. That is, if one company in the group gets into financial trouble, the other firms can be expected to lend a hand. In short, the Mitsui Bank is not assuming 100 percent of the risk when it makes a loan to any one of the companies within this group of twenty-five firms. Here again, the group principle appears to work to good advantage.

Finally, as in other areas, there is the government's willingness to serve as a backstop. When private banks lend out more money than they have on deposit, which apparently happens sometimes, they can turn to the government-owned Bank of Japan for credits to tide them over. This puts the Bank of Japan, together with the Ministry of Finance, in a position to monitor the expansionary process by what is known as "window guidance"—keeping an administrative rein on the practices of private banks. When the Bank of Japan feels that too many industries are expanding too fast, it can simply cut back on credit to the banks, thereby eventually shutting off the flow of capital to the corporations.

The Economy in the International Context

Few countries in the world are self-sufficient; most need to trade with others to secure commodities and products they cannot produce, paying for them by selling their own products. There is a wide variation in the degree to which various nations depend on foreign trade to maintain the health of their economies. A crude measure would be the proportion of the Gross National Product accounted for by exports and imports. In recent years, this proportion in Japan has stabilized somewhere between 18 and 20 percent of the GNP. To some extent this figure understates the importance of foreign trade, because the growth of the GNP increasingly reflects the expansion of the tertiary sector of the economy, the service industries. If one were to allow for this factor, it would probably be true to say that the importance of foreign trade has been steadily increasing in recent years.

Exports are particularly vital to a country like Japan. Certain industries are heavily dependent on foreign markets. In 1968, for example, 40 percent of the precision machinery and 32 percent of the steel produced were exported. There are a large number of large corporations which are export-oriented. The more conspicuous examples, and the percentage of products sold abroad in 1968, are as follows: Sasebo Heavy Industries, 65 percent; Sony, 57 percent; Yamaha Motors, 50 percent; Hitachi Shipbuilding, 44 percent; Sharp Manufacturing, 40 percent; and Mitsui Shipbuilding, 37 percent.

The rapid economic expansion of the 1960s undoubtedly resulted from Japan's success in competing effectively in world markets. American exports grew from roughly $20 billion in 1960 to almost $38 billion in 1969, an increase of 90 percent. In the same period Japanese exports rose from approximately $4 billion to $16 billion, or 400 percent. Much of this increase was concentrated on a limited number of products, including ships, radio and television receivers, watches and clocks, steel, and passenger cars. These products require a high level of technology and large capital investment. They are also more in demand in the industrialized countries than in the developing areas of the world.

The industrialized countries now see Japan as a formidable competitor, as more and more goods labeled "Made in Japan" compete with domestic products. During the last few years Japan has had a favorable balance of trade with the United States, and consequently has acquired a large pool of dollars, a source of some embarrassment. No matter how much one may believe in the efficacy of competition as an abstract principle, few businessmen like competition when it confronts them directly. Already, economic competition has stimulated some anti-Japanese sentiment in the United States. The threat of Japanese competition is likely to lead to more hostile feelings against Japan as time goes on.

A sharp decline in exports, should it come, would markedly affect Japan's economic well-being, because exports not only provide profits for business and jobs for workers, they also earn foreign exchange which can be used to purchase raw materials from abroad. There are few industrialized countries in the world as dependent on imported raw materials for economic survival as Japan. In the United States, increasing concern is being expressed over the "energy crisis" caused by a decline in the domestic supply of oil, leading to the necessity of importing large amounts of foreign oil, which in turn will mean an outflow of more dollars and an unfavorable balance of payments.

Japan has always had to live with an energy crisis, for the country produces only a miniscule amount of oil and natural gas and must import nearly all of it from abroad, mostly from the Middle East. In recent years petroleum has been the most important import item in Japan, and all indications are that the rate of consumption of this important commodity will increase sharply in the future. For understandable reasons, the Japanese have been trying to diversify their sources of supply by helping to finance oil exploration in Indonesia in an attempt to lessen their dependence on a Middle Eastern oil supply subject to political uncertainties. Joint ventures with the Soviet Union to develop Siberian natural gas and oil resources appear to be a real possibility as well. If they are successful Japan will be assured of a continued supply of energy resources for some years to come.

Other important raw material imports include lumber, iron ore, coal, raw cotton, raw wool, wheat, and soybeans. Japan's building industry consumes large amounts of wood, much of which must come from foreign sources, including the United States. In recent years Japan has become a leading exporter of iron and steel, as well as large tankers and other types of vessels. Since the country has no deposits of iron ore or coking coal, these materials, which are vital to a viable steel industry, must be imported, with the United States, Australia, and Canada the most important sources. Although textiles are becoming less important as export items, Japan still has a substantial textile industry which must look to foreign countries for raw cotton and wool. Finally, food products like wheat and soybeans must be purchased abroad, since domestic production does not begin to meet the food needs of the Japanese people.

In short, for its economic survival, Japan must continue to import large quantities of raw materials to keep her industries running, and to export finished goods in order to pay for raw materials and the food she buys. Her profits come from buying relatively cheap raw materials and selling finished goods which can command substantially high price. It is possible to make a great many high-priced precision watches from a ton of iron ore.

The importance the Japanese place on assuring themselves a continuing supply of vital raw materials is underscored by their foreign investment strategy during the last few years. Between 1951 and 1968 almost one-third of their foreign investments went into agricultural, fishing, and mining ventures. Japan has made investments in oil ventures in the Middle East, pulp mills in Alaska, iron ore mines in Australia, and copper and nickel mines in the Philippines, to mention the more conspicuous examples.

Still, compared to a country like the United States, which accounts for about 60 percent of the foreign investments in the entire world, the scale of Japanese foreign investments remains amazingly small: less than 2 percent in 1968, contrasted with Canada's 3.3 percent. Compared to the other advanced industrial countries Japan still ranks low in many respects, despite the fact that in terms of GNP she now ranks third in the world.

The Costs of Economic Growth

There is increasing concern with the quality of life in the advanced industrial countries. It no longer seems desirable to have more and bigger automobiles, refrigerators, and television sets coming off the assembly lines if in the process man's environment is destroyed. It is a sad commentary that today the amount of smog in a city can serve as a convenient index of modernization. Tokyo and other large Japanese cities can lay claim to modernity, for they suffer from smog in no uncertain terms. The chief culprits are the industrial plants which throw out smoke and chemicals from their chimneys, and the ubiquitous automobile.

A country like Japan is particularly vulnerable to atmospheric pollution because of the high population density. Many people are cramped into a small space. A good way to visualize the situation would be to imagine what would happen if half the American people were pushed into the state of California. Fortunately for Japan, car ownership does not begin to approach the scale attained in the United States. In 1968 there were slightly more than five million passenger cars in Japan, in comparison to more than eighty-three million in the United States. One would have to assume that with increased affluence more people will be able to afford cars, and the effects of this trend on air pollution are not hard to imagine.

Already the situation in Tokyo is at times so bad that traffic policemen must duck into police stations periodically for whiffs of oxygen. Vending machines which dispense oxygen are also available in various places for citizens to get more oxygen than is provided by the air they breathe. A few years ago an enterprising department store gave away cans of clean mountain air from Mount Fuji as a publicity stunt.

Recently Ryokichi Minobe, governor of Tokyo, threatened to ban or restrict the use of automobiles in certain parts of the city on those days when smog conditions are particularly bad. He proposed that on alternating days only cars possessing license plates with even or odd numbers be allowed on the streets. Although as yet no large-scale fatalities caused by smog conditions have been reported, people have been hospitalized from time to time. Unless drastic measures are taken soon, air pollution could become intolerable.

The situation with regard to water pollution appears to be no better. One is hard put to find a clear stream or river in Japan. The victims of a widely publicized case in which villagers suffered cadmium poisoning from eating fish caught in a contaminated river took their case to court, seeking damages from the company which had allegedly dumped the chemical into the river. Recently the courts upheld the plaintiffs, and ordered the company to indemnify those who suffered from the poisoning and to correct the situation. This is likely to be a landmark decision. From now on firms guilty of water pollution will be forced to spend large sums for industrial waste treatment or be confronted with damage suits.

In fairness, it should be noted that both industry and government are attempting to cope with air and water pollution. In the summer of 1970 pollution became a national issue when the mass media articulated the concern many people felt. Book publishers, too, joined the fray with an outpouring of books devoted to the problem. In response to this publicity the government established a new agency, the Central Environment Pollution Countermeasures Headquarters, to take the lead in dealing with pollution. Later in 1970 a special session of the Parliament was called to focus on the problem, resulting in the passage of fourteen bills dealing with pollution. In some instances business interests lobbied successfully to weaken the legislative proposals on the grounds that overly stringent regulations would impede economic growth.

Business investment in anti-pollution equipment is increasing. In 1970 some $630 million was spent for equipment designed to collect dust, remove sulphur from waste gases, and treat waste water containing heavy metals. According to projections, expenditures will rise to almost a billion and a half dollars by 1975. No doubt many firms will discover that the need to protect the environment will increase the cost of doing business, making Japanese industry less competitive in world markets. Given the close association that has existed between government and industry, it would appear likely that the government will ultimately use tax money to help private firms fight pollution. Because of its magnitude, even the combined efforts of government and industry might not be sufficient to solve the pollution problem. It may not be possible to have continued economic growth and a pollution-free environment simultaneously.

Another area which will require substantial investment in the future is housing. One would not believe that Japan has the third highest GNP in the world from a look at the way most people are housed. Most foreigners do not notice housing deficiencies because they generally stay in modern Western-style hotels when they visit the country, and do not have much opportunity to see how the average Japanese family lives. By American standards most Japanese live in terribly crowded quarters, especially in the big cities. Traditionally, the people have gotten by with relatively little space because of their life style.

In the past, Japanese dwellings tended to be sparsely furnished, and the rooms were used for multiple purposes. At night the bedding would be rolled out on the straw-matted floor and used for sleeping. Every morning the bedding would be put away and the room could be used for eating, sitting, working, and entertaining. Rooms, moreover, were divided by thin sliding partitions rather than thick walls. This meant that partitions could be removed and the rooms combined when the occasion called for it. It was a flexible system which made maximum use of space.

Nowadays, many people prefer Western-style furniture and modern appliances, with the result that flexibility is drastically reduced. Beds cannot be rolled up and put away in closets like quilts. A room with a bed is now a bedroom, and cannot easily double as a living room. Sitting on sofas and chairs requires much more space than sitting on cushions. The spread of democratic ideas also has meant more stress on individual privacy, so fixed walls rather than moveable, paper-covered partitions are now preferred. This change in living style has led to a demand for more living space. People want their houses and apartments to be substantially larger than they were in the past.

The problem is that space costs money. Housing costs in Japan are phenomenally high. Approximately one-sixth of the housing in the country, and as much as one-half of the housing in the major cities, was destroyed in the war. Losses of this magnitude obviously lead to a housing shortage; in Japan the situation was aggravated by additional factors. As a result of the economic boom there has been a steady migration of workers to the cities, particularly to Tokyo. These migrants needed housing.

A change in family patterns has also affected the housing dilemma. Many young people are no longer willing to live with their parents. They want to be on their own. The ideal setup for young brides, according to a popular saying, is to be "Ie-tsuki, Car-tsuki, Baba-nuki," or "With house, with car, without mother-in-law." Acceptance of this philosophy has created a tremendous demand for housing.

A great deal of construction has been undertaken to meet this demand. In addition to individual homes, large multi-story concrete structures known as *danchi* have gone up, particularly in the suburbs. In some cases entire towns composed of such structures have been built. A little more than a million and a half housing units were constructed in 1969, representing an investment of billions of dollars.

The rising demand for housing, combined with inflation, has pushed building costs up to the point where only the upper middle and upper classes can afford to buy or build individual homes. Land is scarce in

a crowded country like Japan, and land suitable for housing in metropolitan areas rose in price at least tenfold between 1955 and 1968. Since much of the wood must be imported the price of building materials has gone up sharply, to say nothing of labor costs. Today the home buyer must be prepared to spend at least six times his annual income for a small prefabricated house, and since the lending agencies are not likely to loan more than one-half the cost, a large down payment would be required.

Under the circumstances, housing, particularly for urban dwellers, represents a formidable problem. Only a small number of people have been fortunate enough to inherit the family home, or have parents who own a lot large enough to be subdivided. Most people are forced to rent. The government has built large apartment complexes with rentals amounting to only a few dollars a month, and some government workers, especially those in higher positions, have access to this housing. The Japan Housing Corporation, a public agency, also rents and sells space in large apartment buildings, but the demand for these units far outstrips the supply as their prices are lower than the prevailing market.

Many corporations also provide housing for some of their employees. Company-owned units rent at somewhat lower prices than government housing. Persons who do not have access to either government- or company-owned housing must turn to the private rental market, where rents are substantially higher. Some families are forced to rent a room or two in someone's home; others rent units in apartments put up by private developers. Whatever the type of housing, it will not be spacious. Typical dwelling units in the large apartment buildings are those designated "2 DK" and "3 K." A 2 DK unit would consist of a combined dining room-kitchen, a bathroom, a small entry, and two rooms measuring nine feet by twelve feet. The 3K unit would have an additional nine by twelve room. In terms of total space, these units would range from 480 to a little more than 600 square feet. In many cases a family of four would occupy a unit this size. It should be evident from what we have said that the great majority of the Japanese people are forced to put up with housing which would be considered woefully inadequate by contemporary American standards.

What we have said about the quality of housing also applies to the social services in general. Cross-national comparisons in this area are difficult to make, but one might think of a range with the Scandinavian countries at one end, Japan at the other, and the United States somewhere in between. Of the industrialized countries, Sweden probably has gone the farthest to provide a thoroughgoing system of social services extending from the cradle to the grave. To pay for this, the Swedes are heavily taxed. Taxes in Japan, by contrast, are remarkably low. Indeed, economists who have looked into the tax system in Japan have found that the percentage of real income paid in taxes has decreased over the years.

By the same token, social services and public facilities available to the Japanese are on the meager side. Let us consider, for example, the public parks. Washington, D.C., provides forty-five square meters of park space per resident, a relatively high figure; in comparison, Amsterdam provides fourteen, New York twelve, Moscow eleven, and Tokyo only one square meter per person.

Japan's sewage system is also inadequate. London, Stockholm, Manchester, Chicago, and other large cities have installed extensive sewage systems that provide service to virtually every living unit. By comparison, only about 44 percent of the residents of Tokyo have access to an underground sewage disposal system. It is curious, at least from an American point of view, that there should not be loud demands for sewers. As a matter of fact, some years ago Mitaka, one of Tokyo's satellite cities, planned to install an up-to-date sewage disposal system including a large treatment plant. The Mitaka government proposed that the cost be split among the central government, the Mitaka government, and the home owners who would benefit. One would have thought that the residents of Mitaka would have considered this a good deal, but some of them protested, saying they did not want to be assessed for their share.

Another public facility important to city dwellers is a mass transit system. Japanese National Railways and private transportation companies have invested tremendous sums in transportation facilities. Japan has an extensive system of railroads, elevated trains, subways, and buses which operate punctually and efficiently. During the rush hour in Tokyo electric trains ten cars long run on such tight schedules that they have "pushers" on the platforms to push some passengers into the cars and pull others out so that the doors can be closed in time for the trains to meet their schedules. At peak periods trains and subways carry 200 to 300 percent more passengers than their rated capacity.

Despite an ambitious program of subway construction, the increase in the number of passengers is so great that the public transportation system is almost at a breaking point. In fact, Japanese National Railways has gone so far as to commission studies of the physiological effects of overcrowding in trains and subways; perhaps it would have been simpler for them to interview commuters who have to endure the torture every day.

According to a recent story, an American living in Tokyo decided something should be done about the situation. He rounded up some Japanese friends and formed a delegation which visited the management of one of the private lines. The delegation suggested that one or more cars be added to help relieve the congestion. The management replied that they had experimented with more cars, but had found that the trains were still as crowded as ever. The additional cars didn't seem to relieve the overcrowding, so they took them off!

The problem of public transportation in a metropolitan area like Greater Tokyo may well be insoluble. But there are certainly limits to human adaptability and endurance. Perhaps when the trains become sufficiently overcrowded, and the smog sufficiently deadly, people will either die off or move elsewhere; this seems to be the only possibility for relieving congestion in Tokyo. To say that the Japanese have a long way to go toward improving the quality of life is to put it mildly.

A plan which has attracted attention recently is the one put forward by Prime Minister Tanaka in his book, *A Plan for Remodeling the Japanese Archipelago*, which was published in 1972. In the book, Tanaka proposes to disperse the population by using tax incentives to persuade businessmen to build factories in sparsely populated areas in northern Japan and on the island of Shikoku. He envisions some twenty-five new cities to be built, each with a population of approximately 250,000. These cities would be equipped with green belts, recreation areas, and safeguards to keep down pollution. To make this plan a reality, the transportation system would have to be greatly improved.

Tanaka's plan would require the investment of astronomical sums. Ultimately much of this money would come from the people in the form of higher taxes and prices. The question is whether or not they would be willing to forego present income for the sake of improving the quality of life in the future. More than 800,000 copies of Tanaka's book had been sold as of October 1972; its popularity suggests that perhaps the public is now in a mood for change.

It might be possible to interpret the results of the election held on December 10, 1972, as a reflection of this mood for change. Prime Minister Tanaka's ruling Liberal Democratic party managed to maintain a majority of the House of Representatives by winning 271 of the 491 seats, but they lost twenty-six seats.

The Clean Government party, the political arm of the Buddhist organization Sokagakkai, and the Democratic Socialist party also lost seats. The Clean Government party dropped from forty-seven to twenty-nine representatives, while the Democratic Socialists fell from twenty-nine to nineteen. By contrast, the Socialist party gained thirty-one seats, increasing their representation from eighty-seven to 118. The most dramatic increase was recorded by the Communist party, which rose from fourteen to thirty-eight seats, an all-time high for the party. The Communists gained at least one representative in each of the electoral districts in the three cities of Tokyo, Osaka, and Kyoto.

Overall, then, the two radical parties grew at the expense of the moderates. One must be careful, however, not to read too much into these results. In reporting the election returns, the American press stressed the Communist gains, but did not say much about the shifts in votes which brought this about. Actually, an examination of the distribution of the vote shows that shifts in party support were minor. The Liberal Democrats lost a little more than 1 percent of the vote received in the 1969 election. The Socialists made almost no gain in popular vote, and even the Communists won only about 3.5 percent more votes than in 1969. They rose from 7 percent to just under 10.5 percent of the popular vote. By increasing their share of the vote by about one-half, the Communists were able to expand their representation in the House by almost 250 percent.

Quite clearly this increase is a consequence of the vagaries of the Japanese electoral system, in which three, four, or five representatives are elected from each district. In this system election strategy is all-important, for if a party nominates too many candidates the vote will be split among them. Thus, the recent election reflects to some extent a dissatisfaction with the present state of affairs, particularly in the larger cities which suffer from pollution and overcrowding; however, the distribution of the vote suggests that large blocs of voters did not change their political allegiance from one party to another. Political change in Japan is still incremental rather than revolutionary.

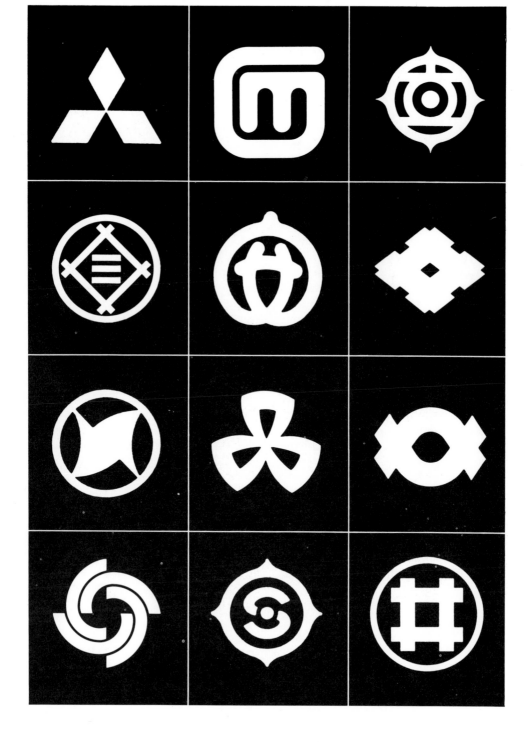

CHAPTER FOUR

WHAT DOES THE FUTURE HOLD?

IN RECENT YEARS speculation about the future has become a popular pastime. More and more people are wondering what kinds of new products we will be using, what sorts of life styles will be likely to prevail, and what the world will be like in the years to come. This preoccupation with the future may be in part a response to the spectacular breakthroughs that have taken place in science and technology, including the series of successful space missions to the moon. It may also be a consequence of the subtle impact of computer technology on our daily lives. The ability of the computer to make complex mathematical calculations quickly and cheaply has enabled government agencies, insurance companies, and other corporations to make projections about the future based on sets of assumptions combined with historical data. In any case, concern with the future is no longer confined to professional planners, but seems to be affecting many segments of the population at large.

Japan's Future Economic Growth

Because of Japan's spectacular economic performance in the postwar period, it is perhaps natural that a certain amount of interest should be focused on her prospects for future growth and the role she is likely to assume in world affairs. To be candid, there is an element of apprehension, even of fear, involved. The prospect of a revival of militarism in Japan, which would be even more formidable in view of her current economic power, has caused some to ask, "Won't what happened in Japan in the 1930s be repeated in the 1980s?" This question and others like it have prompted a number of intellectuals to concern themselves with projections of the likely future course of Japan.

Perhaps the most controversial statement about Japan's future role in world affairs is contained in a widely read book by Herman Kahn, *The Emerging Japanese Superstate: Challenge and Response* (Englewood Cliffs, N.J.: Prentice-Hall, 1970). Kahn predicts that Japanese economic growth will continue into the future, with the result that by the year 2000 Japan's GNP will outstrip that of the United States. He predicts, further, that having attained first rank in the economic arena, Japan will seek to exercise political and/or military power commensurate with her economic clout. Kahn believes there will be powerful pressures to overcome the strong emotional antipathy to nuclear weapons, and as a result Japan will eventually join the nuclear club by producing atomic bombs.

In essence, Kahn projects comparative growth rates of the recent past into the long-range future. The American economy has been growing at a rate of about 4 percent per year. By contrast, the Japanese economy enjoyed about 10 percent growth throughout the 1960s. At a rate of growth of 4 percent per year, an economy would double in about eighteen years; at 10 percent, it would double in about seven years. Thus, it is theoretically possible for Japan to catch up with the United States in a thirty-year period, even though she began from a much smaller base. This sort of projection rests on the assumption that Japan's recent high growth rate would continue indefinitely into the future.

This is a highly dubious assumption. As we showed in the previous chapter, during the 1960s Japan moved from a semi-developed economy to a mature one, with the labor force shifting from the less productive to the more productive sectors. Young workers, both male and female, migrated to the cities where they took jobs in factories equipped with new and efficient machinery. While the role of agriculture in the economy will continue to decline, the transfer of workers from the rural areas to the urban industrial sector cannot go on indefinitely. Already many of the small firms, which are unable to compete with the large corporations in terms of wages and fringe benefits, have found it impossible to recruit all the workers they need. If the country continues to prosper the shortage of labor is bound to become more acute because of recent demographic trends.

According to estimates, the population will continue to grow, but at a rather slow pace of less than 1 percent a year, reaching 117 million or so by 1985. It is expected to reach a peak at about 121 million by the year 2005. Birth control and abortion, which have been legalized in Japan, have helped stem the once vigorous growth in population. The decline in the birth rate has been accompanied by a reduction in the death rate. The combination of declining births and longer life expectancy will naturally affect the age composition of the population. The proportion of individuals between fifteen and sixty-four years of age — the working population — will remain stable during the next twenty years, while the number of people over sixty-five will increase markedly. In 1965 about 6.3 percent of the population was sixty-five or older; by 1985 the figure is expected to rise to about 10 percent.

One can draw several implications from these demographic trends and projections. Labor's bargaining power vis-à-vis management will grow, especially if the labor shortage becomes more serious. Compared to other areas of Asia which are becoming more industrialized—including Taiwan, South Korea, Hong Kong, and Singapore—Japanese wage scales are high, and they are getting higher every year; unions have been able to win annual increases amounting to as much as 15 percent.

Japan is no longer a country of cheap labor, and eventually wages and salaries could match prevailing Western standards. Moreover, Japan will probably not be able to alleviate the shortage of labor by importing foreign labor, as some countries in Western Europe have done in recent years. Japanese labor unions would undoubtedly resist such importation, but more important, the population would not welcome it because of the difficulty in assimilating foreign workers.

Hence, importing foreign workers is not feasible. Instead, industry is more likely to move some production facilities to other countries. There are indications, for example, that Japanese shipbuilders might establish new shipbuilding facilities in Singapore instead of expanding in their own country. In any case, the comparative advantage Japanese industry has enjoyed in the past over its American and European competitors, because of its lower labor costs, will lessen in the future.

In addition to increased wages, the social cost of having to support a growing number of retired people will also rise in the future. By 1975, one out of twelve persons will be sixty-five or older. And the proportion of retired persons will be much higher, due to the customary practices of government and industry which set retirement age at fifty-five. Labor shortage will create pressures to raise the retirement age, but long established customs are not quickly discarded. Since the proportion of older persons will increase in the future at a much faster rate than the working population, the burden of supporting the aged will become heavier. Japanese expenditures for old-age security are still very low, but in the future both individuals and government will have to channel more funds into taking care of the aged.

We have already noted the recent shift in population from the rural areas to the cities. This trend is certain to continue. It is believed that by 1980 almost 80 percent of the population will live in cities and the agricultural population will fall to something like 11 percent of the nation. The steady growth of industrialization and urbanization will accentuate the trend toward occupational specialization and especially the growth of the white-collar class. Within twenty years, persons in management positions, technicians, office workers, and sales personnel will account for about 40 percent of the employed population.

There will also be a steady rise in the educational level of the population. Compulsory education now extends through junior high school, but more and more young people are going on to high school and college. In 1960, 54 percent of those seeking employment were graduates of junior high school, 38 percent had completed high school, and 8 percent were college graduates. By 1975, the proportions are likely to be about 13 percent junior high school graduates, 60 percent high school graduates, and 27 percent college graduates. The educational level of the labor force will rise significantly. This will be an advantage in that the workers will be capable of performing more difficult tasks, but at the same time it will become more difficult to find workers willing to take dull, routine, or physically arduous jobs.

In the last analysis, a key factor in the country's economic future will be what happens to the work ethic—whether or not management and labor will be willing to work as diligently as they have in the past to gain an edge over foreign and domestic competition.

On the face of it there are numerous signs that the work ethic continues strong. One indicator is the reluctance of Japanese workers to take time off for summer vacations. In the Western world a one- or two-week escape from the office or plant during the hot summer months is taken for granted; but this is not the pattern in Japan. In order to help popularize the idea of taking summer vacations, both the Ministry of Labor and MITI have been putting pressure on their staffs to take vacations, with indifferent success. MITI has even taken to assessing fines on employees who fail to take time off. Recent data on the state of affairs in industry are not available, but it has been reported in past years that in a majority of business establishments workers took less than 60 percent of their allotted vacation time.

Another interesting facet of the Japanese work ethic has to do with the number of hours worked per week. Traditionally, the work week has been set at eight hours per day for six days, or forty-eight hours per week, as is specified in the Labor Standards Law. The actual situation varies. The work week is shorter in many establishments where unions have been strong enough to bargain with management. Many firms also schedule overtime work, and even though workers receive only 25 percent extra for working overtime they welcome the opportunity to bring home more money on payday.

In 1965 and 1966 male workers in Japan averaged a little more than fifty-four hours of work per week, in contrast to forty-six in West Germany and forty-four in the United States. The Japanese are quite sensitive to international standards, and this comparison, together with a slowdown in the economy, has recently led to a movement, pushed by the large corporations, for a five-day work week. Ultimately, the shorter week is likely to become standard, but it still appears to be the exception rather than the rule. In the spring of 1972, a Democratic Socialist member of the House of Representatives proposed that the five-day work week be instituted, but this plan was rejected by the Prime Minister's office.

Curiously, many workers reportedly do not favor a shorter work week. This should not be taken to mean that they have a passion for work. As a matter of fact, there are some indications that in Japan, as in many industrialized countries, feelings of job alienation are on the upswing. According to a recent survey among workers in the Japanese Federation of Iron and Steel Workers unions, only about 27 percent of those queried felt positively motivated toward work. About 20 percent said that their work was uninteresting, and about one-half indicated indifference toward their jobs. In essence, Japanese workers are not all that different from their counterparts in other industrialized countries.

It would seem to make more sense to seek explanations of worker attitudes toward vacations and working hours in the nature of the social environment. The basic question is, what does one do with increased leisure time? And this brings up the matter of housing, family structure, and recreational facilities. In most cases, homes and apartments are terribly cramped. If the father is home two days out of seven, this adds to the feeling of crowding. From the family's point of view, it is probably better to have the father working and out of the house.

Also, there is a great difference in activities between a husband and wife. Much of the life of the wage earner is built around the company for which he works. His friends tend to be his business associates. A common sight on Japanese trains is a group of men armed with food and a large bottle of sake, headed somewhere for a vacation. The wife stays home with the children, and her social activities center around visiting and chatting with other mothers in the neighborhood. Families do go on outings and trips together. On Sundays the large downtown department stores are filled with husbands and wives with their small children shopping and having meals in the dining rooms located within the stores. Still, Japanese families typically budget rather small amounts for recreational purposes because there is pressure to save for old age and to educate the young.

Finally, there is the problem of available recreational facilities. There is a relative paucity of parks and cultural facilities in Japan. In 1966 there were only 771 public libraries in the country, or one for every 125,000 persons, and 123 art museums, or one for every 800,000 persons. By contrast, there was one *pachinko* parlor (a shop lined with Japanese-style pinball machines) for every 10,000 persons.

Business firms are much involved in recreational and cultural activities. Most of the gymnasiums and swimming pools are owned and operated by large companies, and approximately 80 percent of all sports clubs, excluding those found in educational institutions, are sponsored by business firms. Some of the sports activities take on a semi-professional coloration, which has the effect of excluding ordinary workers from participation. During the 1964 Olympic Games in Tokyo, for instance, the Japanese were represented by a powerful girls' volleyball team made up of employees of a well-known textile company.

The character of much of the company-sponsored recreation, and the underdeveloped state of cultural facilities intended for the community at large, have deprived large sectors of the population of the opportunity for participation in active forms of recreation and other leisure-time activities. We are inclined to believe that it is this lacuna, together with the housing situation, which accounts for the willingness of the workers to stay on the job for long hours, and not the strong work ethic.

If our interpretation is correct, it would appear that as social conditions change—with greater availability of spacious housing and community recreational facilities—the Japanese penchant for working hard will also change. Increasing worker alienation, together with rising wages brought about by labor shortage, could well act as a brake on continued economic growth.

Another future impediment to economic growth will be uncertainties over export markets. In 1960, on the eve of the period of rapid economic expansion, Japan's portion of world trade was quite small, amounting to 3.2 percent, in contrast to the American share of more than 36 percent. During the 1960s Japan's strong export drive opened up new markets, and her share of world trade was doubled, reaching 6.4 percent in 1970, while the United States' share dropped to 23.1 percent.

Japan has made important gains, but her share could scarcely be called dominant. But even at this level, Japanese export capability is seen as a threat by Western countries, and countermeasures are being instituted. Beginning with President Nixon's decision to devalue the dollar, followed up by subsequent trade negotiations, the United States has tried to restrain the importation of Japanese goods and at the same time increase the sale of American goods in Japan. In September 1972 American pressure caused the Japanese government to rescind the "Buy Japan" order, a ruling in effect since 1963 requiring all government-supported activities to confine their purchases to domestic products whenever they were available.

A recent projection of the economy through the 1970s made by Dr. Saburo Okita, a leading Japanese economist, posits another doubling of Japan's share of world trade by 1980, making it 12.5 percent. The trouble with economic projections of this sort is that they tend to ignore political factors, which are often paramount these days. From a purely economic point of view it is conceivable that Japan could enlarge her share to 12 percent; this would be possible only if the other advanced industrial countries, at whose expense Japanese world trade would expand, would be willing to sit by and permit it. In view of the cries of alarm that arose when the percentage rose from 3 to 6 percent, it seems unrealistic to assume that they would.

On the contrary, increasing pressure will be put on Japan to purchase more goods from abroad. So far, she has succeeded in following a highly protectionist import policy, but she will have to throw open the growing Japanese market to foreign wares if she hopes to continue to export her manufactured goods. Increasing competition will also come from Asian neighbors as South Korea, Taiwan, Hong Kong, Singapore, and Malaysia pursue their industrialization programs. Already, imports of textiles from Asian neighbors have risen from $5.8 million in 1965 to $130 million in 1970. In the future it will be increasingly difficult for Japan to sell goods abroad, while foreign penetration of the domestic market will surely increase.

A third factor impinging on economic growth involves access to raw materials. Since the end of World War II raw material prices have remained relatively low, and those nations producing them have been more than anxious to find foreign buyers. However, the annual consumption of raw materials by many countries has increased so much that now fears are being expressed that the world will run out of vital materials in the not so distant future. This is particularly true with fossil fuels, of which petroleum is the most important. Dr. Okita's projections anticipate that by 1980 Japan will buy about one-half of the iron ore which enters into international trade, and about 20 percent of the petroleum. Since most of the world's oil comes from a few places, of which the Middle East is the most important, Japan will be forced to compete with other oil-hungry industrial powers for a share of a vital but dwindling resource. It may turn out that the Japanese may not be able to acquire as much as one-fifth of the oil sold by 1980. So there are many uncertainties as far as raw materials are concerned.

A fourth factor in Japan's continued economic growth is her reliance on the availability of new technology. So far, foreign firms, including American ones, have been willing to license new inventions and industrial processes to Japanese businesses. But it is questionable that they will continue to do so on the same scale in the future. It has been reported that already some firms have refused to make available new technology unless they are permitted to buy into Japanese companies or enter into joint enterprises. Japan will be forced to spend much more money on research and development in the future, and this will raise business costs.

Finally, the growth of the 1960s was stimulated by the flow of large sums of money into modern productive facilities. Industrial capacity grew, and production processes were also rendered more efficient by the installation of latest model automated equipment. Business, government, and even the public seemed dedicated to the pursuit of a single goal—raising the GNP. The program succeeded much beyond the original expectations; but voices are now being raised, particularly by youth, to question the wisdom of seeking growth for growth's sake. While economic growth has brought a degree of affluence, it has also brought pollution of the environment and urban crowding, and lowered the quality of life in general. Many people are beginning to call for a reordering of priorities. They are in favor of growth, but not at the expense of a seriously deteriorating environment.

The government and many sectors of the public now appear convinced that a substantial investment in infrastructure will be necessary. They realize that more sewage systems will have to be built, roads and transportation systems will have to be expanded, rigorous pollution control will have to be instituted, and, above all, more housing will have to be constructed. In the recent past Japan has been building a little more than one and a half million housing units per year. But this is not enough. The country will need an estimated twenty-four million additional units during the next ten years, an amount roughly equal to

the total number of housing units which now exist. Moreover, about one-half of the housing in existence is considered substandard.

To improve the quality of life, the flow of capital will have to be redirected away from steel mills, automobile plants, and the like to housing, sewers, pollution control, and so on. In the end, the day-to-day life of most of the people will be improved, but the rate of economic growth is likely to be reduced.

The optimistic projections of observers like Herman Kahn and Japanese planners who see a high rate of economic growth continuing indefinitely into the future seem unwarranted. It is likely that the rising cost of labor, decline in the work ethic, difficulties in securing raw materials, and the need to redirect priorities in favor of improving the quality of life will have adverse effects on the economy.

Prospects for Parliamentary Democracy

From time to time Japan's neighbors, particularly those invaded during World War II, have expressed fear of a possible recrudescence of Japanese militarism. The likelihood of a military regime coming to power will probably be related to the strength of the democratic values, institutions, and political processes which have come to dominate the political scene since 1945. Our presumption is that a viable parliamentary democracy ultimately responsive to a peacefully inclined electorate would represent the best barrier against a revival of militarism; an examination of the chances for survival of the parliamentary system serves a useful purpose in our attempt to make predictions about Japan's future.

We must begin by admitting that the democratic ideal is not a product of Japanese history, tradition, or culture. It is, rather, an ideal imported from the West in the course of Japan's modernization. The fact that democracy is not indigenous to Japan should not be taken to mean that it has not been widely accepted. The evidence suggests that today it enjoys genuine support, and it should become even more firmly based with the passage of time, as the number of people socialized into the democratic system increases. In time, they will assume the leadership positions.

Because it is not indigenous to Japan, the democracy that exists there is not a carbon copy of the Western model. For instance, it is not closely associated with individualism. The notion that an individual should have a strongly held set of principles defining what is right and wrong, and that he should act on the basis of these principles as his conscience dictates, is not widely accepted. The Japanese, moreover, are not particularly happy with the principle of majority rule. They prefer to arrive at decisions based on consensus and unanimity after a maximum of consultation among all parties involved. In fact, when the ruling political party pushes through legislation because it has more votes, the opposition may bring forth charges of "tyranny of the majority." Unanimous agreement cannot be attained in large bodies most of the time, and so the wishes of the majority do, in fact, become the rule. In choosing its president, who then becomes the prime minister, the Liberal Democratic party follows the majority principle. The candidate with the most votes in the convention wins.

Even though the Japanese conception of democracy may have different nuances than the system we are accustomed to in this country, it is nevertheless true that the way politics has operated since 1945 has been essentially democratic. Political parties are free to organize, put up candidates, and appeal to the electorate for support. Even the Communist party openly solicits support and manages to place its leaders in elective positions. Diverse political opinions are publicly expressed and the press is more often than not hostile toward the government. Elections are held periodically; all citizens who are willing to take the time to go to the polls are able to vote.

It is not a perfect system, for, as in other democratic systems, it requires large sums of money to run for office. Nevertheless, Japan is a parliamentary democracy, and no government which willfully and consistently outrages the electorate is likely to endure long. I think it is a fair assumption that much of the time most of the influential people in Japan have tacitly, if not actively, supported the government in power and the rules and conventions by which it operates. The question is, will the existing parliamentary democracy continue into the future?

Even a cursory survey of the types of political regimes that exist in the world today would show that viable parliamentary democracies are in the minority. Democracy is a fragile system, and certain conditions must be present before it can flourish and survive.

First of all, there must be an underlying social consensus, a wide sharing of attitudes, values, historical traditions, and a sense of belonging to a political community. This does not mean that no cleavages can exist, for there are bound to be social differentiations and conflicts of one sort or another; but the cleavages must not be such that they split the political community in a fundamental way. History has shown that certain kinds of differences are particularly difficult to bridge. One of these is religion, as daily newspaper dispatches from Northern Ireland so tragically and eloquently demonstrate. Fortunately, Japan does not have a religious problem.

Another basic cleavage is related to ethnic differences. Examples are the recent upheaval in Pakistan leading to the establishment of Bangladesh, and the withdrawal of Singapore from the Malaysian Federation owing to the inability of the Malays and persons of Chinese descent to live and work together within one nation. The Japanese, being a homogeneous people, do not suffer from racial and ethnic hostility.

Finally, there is the concept of class conflict stressed by Marxists. That social classes exist and, more important, that people consciously think of themselves as belonging to one class or another, cannot be denied. But to some extent the strong group orientation in Japanese society mitigates against the development of a class conflict situation; horizontal ties, a prerequisite for class solidarity, tend to be weaker than vertical ties between superiors and subordinates. In a survey of workers in a large industrial firm, respondents were asked four questions relating to support of left-wing parties, commitment to the working class, labor-management conflict, and the role of labor unions in promoting working class solidarity—all questions which anyone espousing Marxist ideology would be expected to answer in the affirmative. Yet only two percent of the workers interviewed did so.

Perhaps the most important cleavage affecting Japanese politics since 1954 concerns the so-called "reverse course" concept and the foreign policy associated with it. Conservatives who rule the country periodically decry the "excesses" of the occupation and propose to revive some of the practices of the prewar period, such as building up the military forces, centralizing the police system, and reestablishing civics courses in schools to inculcate patriotism. Any attempt to turn the clock back is bound to arouse the ire of the opposition forces and they have even resorted to violence. The memories of repression in the prewar period are still strong among those in the ranks of the opposition today. At the same time, political wrangling is not without its ironic moments. The Leftist forces oppose the military alliance with the United States on the grounds that American foreign policy is imperialistic. Yet they staunchly and consistently defend the American-written Constitution; the conservatives, who are pro-American, would like to change it.

The response of the conservatives to the reverse-course issue has been to avoid proposals and actions which blatantly smack of reviving the past. While in office between 1960 and 1964, the late Prime Minister Hayato Ikeda adopted a "low posture" policy aimed at reducing conflict with the opposition. His successor, Eisaku Sato, who resigned in 1972, was less conciliatory but tended to continue that policy.

As a result, while both the government and the opposition may exchange angry words, considerable accommodation has been attained.

A good indicator of this is the voting record in the most powerful elective body, the House of Representatives. During the 1968 session a total of ninety-five government-sponsored bills were passed. The opposition Democratic Socialist and Clean Government parties voted with the government more than 80 percent of the time; the Socialist party, the leading opposition party, voted in favor of two-thirds of the bills. Even the Communist party voted for 25 percent of the bills. A widely shared feeling of belonging to the political community appears to overshadow those conflicts which exist in contemporary Japan.

A second prerequisite for the long-term survival of parliamentary democracy is the establishment of legitimacy. The parliamentary regime must be perceived to be legitimate by both members of the elite and the mass public. Despite the political demonstrations which have erupted, there is no evidence of deeply felt rejection of the system. There are a few revolutionary youth organizations that appear to shun all forms of authority, but their membership is quite small and they do not appear to command the respect of the public. Political scientists point out that the sense of legitimacy tends to be strengthened by the passage of time. In every system, the young are socialized into the political arrangements that prevail. The larger the number of generations socialized into a parliamentary system and the longer it has been in operation, the better its chances for survival in the face of adversity.

Compared to some Western democracies, Japanese democracy is still young. Since 1945, the Japanese have not been confronted by a severe crisis—a serious economic depression, for instance—so the commitment to the parliamentary system has never been tested. In this sense its durability is unsure; but the evidence suggests that there is reason to be more optimistic than pessimistic about its future. It should be noted that the nature of the international environment would be an important influence. The likelihood of parliamentary democracy surviving would be significantly decreased if the world moved in the direction of militant nationalism, protectionism in foreign trade, and intense hostility among nations.

A third consideration in trying to assess the future of parliamentary democracy is the attitude of the public toward political leaders. There is an affective side to politics, too. Do the Japanese people generally like and respect those in political office? For the most part, no. Politicians and parties do not evoke among the public feelings of respect, trust, or affection. Why this should be so is not altogether clear, but it is very likely related to the preference for group harmony and consensus. The ideal image of government is one that is impartial, fair, and works consistently for the public good. But democratic politics promotes an atmosphere of partisanship in which contending politicians and parties strive to maximize their support among the electorate. And the side that wins will favor its allies instead of assuming an impartial stance. One of the problems of Japanese democracy is that the group orientation tends to stifle the development of voluntary political associations which could oppose special interests and contribute to the promotion of the public good. A democracy that does not nurture trust in its leaders leaves something to be desired.

One consequence of this negative attitude toward leaders and parties is political apathy. Various studies suggest that the majority of the Japanese have relatively little interest in politics. However, the voting rate has been high. In the 1950s almost 75 percent of the eligible voters turned out for the House of Representatives elections, but during the 1960s the voting rate declined to 68.5 percent in the 1969 national election, still high by American standards. The turnout is influenced by the notion that voting is a duty, and by community and social pressures to vote.

The decline of voting among youth is particularly pronounced. Government surveys show that in 1952 about 15 percent of those in their twenties did not vote, but by 1969 this figure had nearly doubled, reaching 29 percent. As might be expected, youth who do not bother to vote are more frequently those who do not identify with a particular political party. This would suggest an ebbing of partisanship and political commitment. The dominance of the conservative Liberal Democratic party election after election may be a factor. The youth who want to see a change but realize that their votes are not likely to bring it about feel frustrated.

Perhaps the most important reason for increasing political apathy among youth is the tendency toward privatization, or a tendency to seek self-gratification rather than public goals. This is not a recent development. National surveys repeated over the past fifteen years suggest that there has been a persistent trend with every new age group in the direction of self-centeredness. More and more youth state that their purpose in life is to lead a comfortable existence which will provide maximum opportunity to indulge their individual preferences and tastes and a minimum of concern with social and political problems.

At this point we can only speculate as to why Japanese youth should opt for privatization. They grew up in an atmosphere of increasing affluence, where jobs were plentiful and the standard of living rose steadily. They had the economic means to engage in the pursuit of pleasure. The older generation, which was socialized during a period of economic scarcity and is still bound by an ethic which stresses individual sacrifice for the collective good, continues to take social responsibility more seriously. Apathy and privatization are inimical to a healthy and viable democracy. But perhaps we can take comfort in the knowledge that the youth of Japan is not hell-bent on reviving militarism and supporting an aggressive foreign policy.

Before concluding the discussion of the future of parliamentary democracy, it may be useful to attempt a trial balance. One would be forced to acknowledge that because it was imported from the West democracy is not yet firmly rooted in Japanese culture. There are also other features — lack of affection for political leaders and growing apathy, especially among youth — which throw some doubt on the future viability of this system. On the other side of the ledger, we may point to the absence of deep-seated cleavages and the existence of an underlying social consensus. There are no issues which are not bargainable. Nevertheless, Japanese democracy has never been put to a severe test. It would seem likely that a test, should it come, would originate in the external environment. It is here, therefore, that we will next turn our attention.

Foreign Relations and Policy

Japanese foreign policy since 1945 may be summarized quite succinctly: it is pro-American, depending on the United States nuclear umbrella for defense against external attack; it is passive rather than active; and since its underlying motivation is to promote economic growth, it aims to cultivate friends and avoid making enemies. Not surprisingly, it is vague, sometimes inconsistent, and always weak-kneed. Why such a foreign policy emerged historically is not difficult to understand. In 1945 Japan was a defeated country, friendless and judged guilty of aggression by the world community. As a result of defeat the empire was dismantled, the armed forces demobilized, and the country subjected to a military occupation. The Japanese had little recourse but to accept American direction. During the occupation American policy gradually evolved from punishment and reform to rehabilitation and finally to the elevation of Japan to the position of a junior partner in a military alliance.

In the course of this evolution a patron-client relationship was established between the two countries. This relationship continues, although under increasing strain. The two most important facets of this relationship have to do with national security and economics.

From the Japanese point of view, the strongest and virtually only threat to their national security has come from the Soviet Union. Real-

izing that a meaningful system of security against the Soviet Union based solely on their own efforts was not feasible, they chose to rely on the United States to defend them. In return they had to grant military bases to the United States and to agree in general to act in concert with American foreign policy. American leaders hoped that the Japanese would take an active anti-Communist stance and cooperate with American efforts to contain the spread of Communist influences in Asia.

The Japanese have cooperated in this endeavor, but only passively; they have resisted pressure from the United States to rearm more vigorously and help take over the American role of policeman in the Western Pacific. American military and economic aid, initial American sponsorship in reestablishing markets throughout the world, and, perhaps most important, the opening up of the vast and immensely rich American market to Japanese goods have helped her to achieve an economic miracle. Continued accessibility to the American market is obviously essential if Japan is to keep prospering and this fact is widely recognized in Japan. Thus, the United States exercises a powerful attraction and nothing short of a drastic political upheaval is likely to lead the Japanese to turn their backs on this powerful ally.

Portents of change are to be found in many quarters. A common assumption is that as an aftermath of the Vietnam war the United States will be less anxious to get involved in Asian politics. Even a neo-isolationism cannot be completely ruled out. The waning of American influence in Asia, even if on a small scale, has profound implications for all Asian countries, but especially for a country like Japan which continues to be dependent on the United States for protection from external attack.

There are changes within Asia itself. The efforts of Communist China, now armed with nuclear weapons, to reenter the world community and to develop economic and diplomatic relations with the United States suggest that a new era in Asian politics is upon us. It is made more complex by rivalry and conflict between the two great Communist powers, China and the Soviet Union. Japan will be forced to respond to these changes in the external environment. We can develop a better perspective on the type of response likely to come if we think in terms of a series of hypothetical positions the Japanese could adopt vis-à-vis the world community.

The first hypothetical possibility would be an all-out internationalist position. This, in my view, would be an attractive and logical response given Japan's situation and needs. Economically, the country needs to import raw materials at favorable prices and to sell manufactured goods in sufficient volume to pay for imports. This presupposes a world made up of friendly and cooperative nations dedicated to the principles of free trade. The Japanese should be working in a positive fashion for this sort of world order. This would mean that they would take the lead in setting an example by removing protectionist policies at home. It would also mean working in a positive manner for international cooperation, for peaceful relations among nations and peoples, and for the emergence of a just world order.

In terms of national security, it would mean advocating worldwide disarmament and consistently opposing military blocs and defensive alliances. If the Japanese adopted the internationalist position, they would have to take the lead in disarmament in order to set the right moral example. They would have to play down nationalism and opt for a more cosmopolitan way of life. They would have to become fluent in foreign languages and learn to be at home in other cultural settings.

There are some signs that the Japanese sense the attractiveness of this position. For instance, the Japanese do not have close ties with the Swiss, yet in polls in which respondents are asked to name the country which Japan should use as a model, Switzerland ranks high (as does the United States). The idea of a lightly armed, neutral nation on friendly terms with everyone has appeal. Another indication is what Zbigniew Brzezinski called living up to the image of the "good boy" in his book, *The Fragile Blossom*. The Japanese have engaged in international "do-goodism" by supporting the United Nations, giving increasing amounts of foreign aid, and being generous in international humanitarian and relief activities.

However, the adoption of an internationalist role would go against the historical and cultural traditions of the Japanese. It is hard to imagine the Japanese, given their parochial orientation, becoming cosmopolitan citizens of the world. It would mean, in essence, giving up their national identity. No matter how logical or attractive the internationalist position, it is not likely to be adopted in any significant way.

A second hypothetical position would be to actively promote some sort of Asian regionalism. This would mean exploiting the geographic, cultural, and racial affinities the Japanese have with their Asian neighbors. In an economic sphere Japan already has attained an imposing leadership position in Asia. Its GNP in 1969 was more than three times larger than that of Communist China and all of Southeast Asia combined. Japan is now the most important trading partner for a majority of the Asian nations, accounting for nearly one-fifth to two-fifths of their total foreign trade. Japan also has large-scale investments in South

Korea, Taiwan, Singapore, Thailand, and Malaysia, and much of her foreign aid has been directed to Southeast Asia. At the Ministerial Conference for the Development of Southeast Asia held in Djakarta in May 1970, Japan pledged to give a total of $4 billion in aid by 1975.

Asian nations are already doing substantial business with Japan and the volume may very well increase in the future. Not everyone is completely happy with the strong position Japan has gained. Complaints are heard about Japanese aggressiveness in doing business, about the hard bargains they drive, and about their clannishness. A Thai is said to have remarked, "They fly in on Japan Air Lines, are met by Japanese guides, ride to Bangkok in Japanese buses, stay in Japanese hotels, and eat and drink in Japanese restaurants, all staffed by Japanese." And there is certainly no evidence that Asians would welcome Japan if she assumed a leadership position in political and military affairs. The prewar attempt to establish a "Greater East Asia Co-Prosperity Sphere" through military force is still remembered in Eastern Asia and no one wants to see that phase of recent history repeated.

The problem with the notion of Asian regionalism is that Asia does not have the basic sense of unity which characterizes the Western world. The countries of Western Europe, together with their offshoots in the New World, Australia, and New Zealand, share a common historical and cultural tradition going back to the Greeks and Romans, and a common set of religious and ethical values. The modern European state system emerged historically from a universal community, the Holy Roman Empire.

This is not the case in Asia. There is no single Asian civilization as such but rather several civilizations: Chinese, together with its Japanese offshoot; Indian; and Islamic. Nor is there a dominant religion. Buddhism, Hinduism, Islam, Shinto, Christianity, and a large number of local religions vie for the allegiance of millions of Asians.

Aside from the hostility Asians would feel toward Japan's assuming a leadership position, the Japanese themselves probably would not want it. Most Japanese do not identify with their fellow Asians. Among foreign peoples the Japanese most admire, Americans and West Germans rank high, while Chinese, Indians, and other Asians rank much lower. The number of Japanese who study English must far outnumber those who are studying other Asian languages. Although Japan is geographically a part of Asia she is much closer to the advanced industrial nations of the West in terms of economic organization, science and technology, and life styles. If one were to take a series of indices—urbanization, GNP, number of automobiles per capita, telephones and newspaper circulation per capita, medical facilities, and school attendance, for instance—Japan would align with the Western group rather than with the countries of the Third World.

All this suggests that Japan may belong within the Western grouping of nations. Yet because the Japanese are racially, historically, and culturally outsiders, it is highly unlikely they will be fully accepted by the Western club in the near future. Despite the fact that the United States is a Pacific power and much is said of the future importance of the Pacific area, American attention is mostly fixed on Europe. The number of students studying the Japanese language in colleges and universities in this country is infinitesimally small compared to the number engaged in learning French, German, and Spanish. The amount of space devoted to Japan in American daily newspapers is amazingly small. The same could be said of the amount of time radio and television programs devote to Japan. Japan does attract a certain number of tourists every year and there are some Americans interested in Japanese flower arrangement, karate, and Zen meditation; but the number of Americans who have profound understanding of Japanese civilization is pitifully small.

The fourth and final hypothetical option open to Japan is the policy of "going it alone." Such a policy would ride on the rising tide of nationalism which is now apparent. Success in the economic field has helped overcome some of the feelings of inferiority induced by defeat in World War II. A sense of pride and confidence is being restored. As a result the inequality in status implicit in the security treaty with the United States will be resented increasingly as time goes on. It might be tempting to get rid of all defensive pacts, to try to solve the national security problem by relying only on one's own armed forces, and to look inward and backward both intellectually and culturally.

After all, there was an interlude in the 1930s when Japan, caught up in a wave of ultra-nationalism, closed the door to foreign influences, and built up its own defenses. But it is difficult to see how Japan could survive as a viable entity if it withdrew in this manner. It simply does not have the natural resources necessary to keep the industrial machine functioning. It cannot live in splendid isolation.

When we examine recent Japanese foreign policy, traces of all the foregoing hypothetical options may be found. Foreign policy at any one point in time represents a composite of these options, and since they are not blended into a harmonious whole Japanese foreign policy appears to be vacillating and inconsistent. Over a period of time the mix changes and one position seems to dominate the others.

In the fall of 1972 Prime Minister Tanaka made an unprecedented journey to Peking and announced the establishment of diplomatic relations with the People's Republic of China. This represented a sharp break from the policies of his predecessors, who had consistently followed the American lead with respect to Chinese politics by supporting the Republic of China in Taiwan politically and economically. For a long time both elite and public opinion in Japan has been divided over which of the two Chinese regimes should get the nod. Actual policy represented a compromise: using the handy formula of "separation of politics and economics," the Japanese recognized Chiang Kai-shek's government and on that basis engaged in trade and made substantial investments in Taiwan. Concurrently, the Japanese did business with the Communists ($825 million in 1970).

Normally one would have expected the Japanese to wait for the United States to make the switch from Taiwan to Mainland China; but in this case the Japanese chose to lead rather than follow. The impetus for taking this bold step was the so-called "Nixon shock." President Nixon apparently did not consult Japanese leaders about his proposed visit to Peking but merely informed them about it a short time before the public announcement was made. Some time later he followed this with a new economic policy which ultimately forced an upward revaluation of the yen, thereby putting Japanese exporters at a disadvantage. Although well-informed people in Japan understood why President Nixon felt impelled to do what he did, the steps he took offended many. The Japanese responded by moving rapidly toward the establishment of closer relations with the Peking government. In terms of the analytical scheme we have proposed, the leadership-in-Asia position and, to a lesser extent, the nationalistic option have been strengthened at the expense of the policy of close association with the United States and the other advanced industrial countries.

The prime impetus for shifts in Japanese foreign policy could come from the external environment. The Japanese tend to respond to changes rather than to initiate them. A response in the area of foreign policy would be related to the interplay of domestic politics as well. The adoption of a new policy toward Communist China, for instance, was facilitated by Tanaka's election to the prime ministership. His success in the election was undoubtedly influenced by growing dissatisfaction over his predecessor's poor relations with Peking.

We would suppose that if recent trends in domestic politics continue and the electoral support for the Liberal Democratic party declines further, foreign policy will become even less decisive. In any case, the days when Japanese foreign policy makers walked one to two steps behind American policy appear to be gone, perhaps forever.

The Problem of Defense

If Japan will go her own way in policy matters in the future, what will happen to the matter of national security? Will Japan get out from under the American nuclear umbrella? Nothing drastic is likely to happen until after 1975. As far as the prospects for rapid arms buildup are concerned, the most reasonable expectation would be that the Japanese will increase their security forces gradually.

It should be recognized that there are those in the United States who would like to see Japan become strong militarily so she can "do her share" to prevent the spread of Communist influence in Asia. Given the Nixon doctrine of Asians defending themselves with American arms, it may even become official American policy to push in this direction.

The Japanese are not likely to respond favorably to such pressure. First of all the political opposition has consistently fought efforts to rearm, even on a small scale. There are no signs that the Socialist, Communist, and Clean Government parties have had a change of heart on this question. Any government which seeks to expand the armed forces in Japan at an accelerated pace will have to cope with political obstruction and probably a series of protest demonstrations. The opposition forces, by leading the fight against rearmament, are likely to gain considerable support from the mass public. Pacificism still remains strong in Japan, and it appears to be deeply rooted. A good indicator of pacifist sentiment is the difficulty the armed forces have persistently encountered in recruiting enough volunteers to bring the army, navy, and air force up to authorized strength. Not many young men want to serve.

Large-scale rearmament is also likely to hurt Japan's image abroad, particularly in Asia. On numerous occasions Chinese Communist leaders have publicly voiced fears of a revival of Japanese imperialism backed by military might. Similar sentiments have been expressed by leaders in a number of Southeast Asian countries. The decision to increase aid to Asian countries in the future would suggest that the Japanese do value the friendship and goodwill of their neighbors. Calculations about what other Asians are likely to think certainly must enter into the making of foreign policy.

The impetus to invest large sums in armaments is also affected by a nation's perceptions of the need to do so. The trend toward detente which appears to characterize world politics in recent years has reduced pressure on Japan's leaders to strengthen defenses. Tension between the United States and the two Communist giants, China and the Soviet Union, has lessened. Russo-Japanese relations have improved and the possibilities of Japanese involvement in the development of Siberia appear good. The Japanese also look forward to more friendly relations with Peking.

For many years the situation on the Korean peninsula represented a source of anxiety, but recent developments suggest that the high level of hostility between South and North Korea may be drastically reduced and that some sort of accommodation eventually may be reached. The world as seen from Tokyo certainly must appear to be moving in the direction of peace and friendship rather than in the direction of hostility and war. At the moment the Japanese probably feel less threatened than at any time since 1945. If this is so it would mean that they would have even less incentive than before to rearm on a large scale.

Given their geographic location and the awesome destructive power of present-day weapons, the Japanese may well have concluded, perhaps unconsciously, that there is no way they can assure their survival should a nuclear holocaust erupt. I am not aware of much public discussion of this point, but some consideration of the ultimate possibilities of survival in a nuclear war must enter into Japanese calculations about the desirability of increased military strength. The great advantage that the continental countries—the United States, the Soviet Union, China, and India—have over Japan is space. Their sheer size makes it unlikely that they will be wiped off the face of the earth in one blow.

Japan by contrast is small and, worse still, her industries are concentrated in a narrow belt extending from Tokyo through Osaka and into northern Kyushu. This industrial belt would present an easy target for missiles fired from the Asian mainland. Japan's industrial capability could be wiped out in a matter of minutes. Whether the Japanese could ever erect a foolproof defense system against such a missile attack is highly problematical. Under the circumstances it might be natural to take a fatalistic approach, and fatalism is one of the cultural traits of the Japanese. Their attitude seems to be: why make a great effort at national defense if in the end you are bound to lose?

Having stated arguments as to why Japan is not likely to rearm on a large scale, counter-pressures must be acknowledged. Japan does not have a large defense establishment, but a defense agency does exist and like all government agencies it has a vested interest in expanding—in gaining larger appropriations and more personnel, prestige, and political clout. Unlike defense departments in many other countries, it does not have large and powerful organizations like veterans' groups which could be mobilized to lobby on its behalf. Nevertheless, the defense agency has managed to get larger budgets and newer and more powerful weapons.

But the scale of defense spending has remained small by international standards, somewhere between one-fourth and one-tenth of what other nations are spending. Although Japan does not yet have anything approaching an industrial-military complex, a number of large corporations have involved themselves in defense work. Initially the Japanese procured much of their military hardware from the United States, but they have steadily converted to domestic production, often using American technology under licensing arrangements. The defense contractors would also like to develop foreign markets. If Japanese defense spending were to increase they could achieve larger volume and bring down unit costs, making it easier to penetrate foreign markets. These counterpressures are not strong, but they do exist and will be reflected in slowly rising defense budgets. However, if the economy continues to grow the proportion spent on arms will remain quite small.

No discussion of national defense would be complete without some mention of nuclear arms. Observers like Herman Kahn have suggested that Japan will acquire nuclear arms in the future. Japan has the capital and technology to build nuclear arms if she so desires. In addition, the strong emotional antipathy toward atomic weapons that once existed has waned, particularly among the younger generation. For a long time no one dared discuss in public even the possibility of Japan's acquiring such weapons, but that taboo has disappeared. The reluctance with which Japan signed the Nuclear Non-Proliferation Treaty is another factor which would lead one to conclude that Japan might choose to join the nuclear club.

In actuality that probability is rather low. Building a nuclear arsenal would be expensive and would lead to internal political turmoil. Moreover, Japan does not have a domestic supply of uranium so this crucial raw material would have to come from foreign sources. More important, the usefulness of nuclear arms might be limited. Everyone hopes they will never be used. It is highly unlikely that Japan would acquire nuclear arms unless a number of middle-ranking powers—West Germany, India, and Israel, for instance—came to possess them. In that event, Japan might choose to follow suit. Japan might be a follower, but she would not be a leader in nuclear proliferation. Perhaps we can conclude that this is indeed a fortunate situation for the sake of world peace.

Concluding Remarks

Japan has begun to play an active role in the world community only recently. For much of the time in the past the Japanese have lived in relative isolation; in the modern world they can no longer cut themselves off from other nations. Japan must increase her interaction with other countries. This will lead to a certain amount of tension and conflict given the parochial nature of her history and culture. The problem is aggravated by the inability of the Japanese to define clearly for themselves the role their country should play in contemporary world politics.

That the Japanese are capable of making a significant contribution to the well-being of mankind is self-evident. As an advanced industrial nation Japan shares many problems with the United States and the countries of Western Europe, including pollution of the environment, urban overcrowding, and industrial conflict. All parties would have much to gain by working together to solve these problems.

As an Asian nation, Japan also has a special responsibility to help her less developed neighbors. She can do this via direct economic aid, technological training, capital investments, and by opening up the growing Japanese market to goods produced in Asia.

Crucial to any increase in mutually satisfying interaction among nations is the problem of understanding. The Japanese people and their leaders must make a concerted effort to learn about the cultural values, social systems, and national aspirations of other countries. Similarly, other nations should try to understand the Japanese. This is particularly important for Americans; as the world's leading nation, the United States vitally affects the welfare of the Japanese in the policies it pursues.

READER'S GUIDE

Japanese publishers put out tens of thousands of books each year, enough to make Japan one of the world's leaders in publishing output. There is a large body of material written by Japanese scholars, essayists, and journalists on their own history, culture, and society. My primary responsibility when I first came to Stanford fresh from graduate school was to build up the Japanese Collection in the Hoover Library. Over the years I have read, studied, and skimmed countless volumes and articles written in Japanese; some of the information and ideas gathered in that process have found their way into the pages of this book.

In this guide, however, I will suggest only sources written in English. I have tried to choose more recent publications, and, where possible, those available in paperback editions.

Mythology, History, and Religion

Readers interested in Japanese mythology may wish to look at a new translation of the *Kojiki* ("Record of Old Things") by Donald L. Philippi (Princeton and Tokyo: Princeton University Press and University of Tokyo Press, 1969). The *Kojiki* was completed in A.D. 712, and is an authoritative source, but some may find it tedious to read. A more readable book, which has the additional virtue of providing information on Shinto, is Jean Herbert's *Shinto: At the Fountain-head of Japan* (New York: Stein and Day, 1967). This work covers the material in the *Kojiki* and also touches on temples, festivals, and methods of worship.

A more concise work on religion, which is also broader in scope, is *Folk Religion in Japan: Continuity and Change* by Ichiro Hori (Chicago: University of Chicago Press, 1967). The text is based on the

Haskell Lectures the author delivered at the University of Chicago in 1965. He includes a discussion of shamanism in Japanese religion.

In the field of history, the literature is extensive, so I have been forced to make some rather arbitrary selections. Professor John W. Hall of Yale has produced a readable and scholarly book, *Japan: From Prehistory to Modern Times* (New York: Dell Publishing Co., 1970), which is available in paperback. He has devoted more space to the earlier history than to the period after 1850. Those interested in looking at the impact of the West on Japanese civilization may wish to read *The Western World and Japan* by the late Sir George Sansom (New York: Alfred A. Knopf, 1950). Sir George was commercial attaché to the British Embassy in Tokyo for many years (and a consultant-professor at Stanford after his retirement), but managed to find time to write several scholarly works on Japanese history. He is noted for his urbane and witty style.

There are many specialized monographs on twentieth-century Japan, but no work which presents an overall view. A handy survey which covers both Japan and China is *Modern East Asia: Essays in Interpretation*, edited by James B. Crowley (New York: Harcourt, Brace and World, 1970, paperback edition). It contains six essays by leading scholars covering the Tokugawa and Meiji periods, party rule between 1905 and 1932, Japanese imperialism, Japanese expansion in East Asia, and economic recovery since 1945.

An important work on militarism and the Japanese form of fascism in the 1930s is *Thought and Behavior in Modern Japanese Politics* by Masao Maruyama (London: Oxford University Press, 1969, paperback edition). Professor Maruyama is one of Japan's leading theorists. This volume contains English translations of several of his notable essays on militarism in Japan.

Finally, for the history of the postwar period, I would recommend the recently published book, *100 Million Japanese: The Postwar Experience* (Tokyo and Palo Alto: Kodansha International, 1972). The author, Professor Masataka Kosaka, a young scholar and frequent contributor to Japanese magazines, teaches at Kyoto University. He gives a vivid picture of postwar Japan.

Society and Culture

The best brief account of group structure and operation is Chie Nakane's *Japanese Society* (Berkeley: University of California Press, 1970, paperback edition). Miss Nakane, a social anthropologist, is the only woman on the faculty of the prestigious University of Tokyo. My students tell me they have learned a great deal from reading her book. Another book by the same title, *Japanese Society* by Takeshi Ishida (New York: Random House, 1971, paperback edition), approaches the subject from a different angle. Professor Ishida, a political scientist, also teaches at the University of Tokyo. His book gives us an idea of how a Japanese intellectual sees his own society.

A more specialized work which contains some interesting studies is *Aspects of Social Change in Modern Japan*, edited by Ronald P. Dore (Princeton: Princeton University Press, 1967, paperback edition). Included are essays on social mobility, village life, collective bargaining, and Japanese gangs. A short essay by Dr. L. Takeo Doi, a Japanese psychiatrist, discusses Japanese feelings of dependency and relates them to Japan's historical development.

Another approach to Japanese society is through village and urban studies. Of the various village studies available, the most comprehensive is *Village Japan* by Richard K. Beardsley, John W. Hall, and Robert E. Ward (Chicago: University of Chicago Press, 1959). The book is the result of a group effort by faculty members at the University of Michigan. Although it is now a bit outdated, Ronald P. Dore's *City Life in Japan* (Berkeley: University of California Press, 1958, paperback edition) is a classic study of urban life. Professor Dore, a British sociologist, lived in a ward in Tokyo during the early 1950s. His observations are recorded in his book. A more recent work on the urban white-collar class is *Japan's New Middle Class* by Ezra F. Vogel (Berkeley: University of California Press, 1963, paperback edition). Professor Vogel, who teaches at Harvard, also obtained his data through observation of urban life in Japan.

Politics and the Economy

There are numerous books on Japanese government and politics, but the one I would like to recommend is my own, *Japanese Politics: Patron-Client Democracy* (New York: Alfred A. Knopf, 1972, paperback edition). Since modesty inhibits me from extolling its virtues, I will merely say it is the most recent, and therefore most up-to-date, study available. Readers who would like to get a picture of practical Japanese politics might look at Nathaniel B. Thayer's *How the Conservatives Rule Japan* (Princeton: Princeton University Press, 1969).

As for economic developments, there is a wealth of material on both historical and contemporary periods in *The State and Economic Enterprise in Japan*, edited by William W. Lockwood (Princeton: Princeton University Press, 1965, paperback edition). This large volume contains essays by both American and Japanese scholars. A succinct account of the economy, with emphasis on policy, is Kozo Yamamura's *Economic Policy in Postwar Japan* (Berkeley: University of California Press, 1967). Professor Yamamura, who teaches at the University of Washington, argues that the economic democracy fostered by the occupation has fallen victim to economic growth. A book containing useful insights for those involved in business transactions with Japanese firms is *Doing Business in Japan*, edited by Robert Ballon (Tokyo: Sophia University-Tuttle, 1967). A view of the corporate world as seen by manual workers is presented in *Japanese Blue Collar: The Changing Tradition* by Robert E. Cole (Berkeley: University of California Press, 1971). Professor Cole actually worked in two factories in Japan, and is able to discuss in great detail how workers relate to other workers and to management.

Foreign Relations and Policy

In addition to Herman Kahn's book, which was mentioned in Chapter Four, there are several recently published books which attempt to forecast Japan's probable role in world politics during the coming decades. *Forecast for Japan: Security in the 1970s*, edited by James W. Morley of Columbia University (Princeton: Princeton University Press, 1972), is a collection of essays by specialists on Japan. Professor Morley argues in his concluding essay that the Japanese would like to see the United States maintain its military readiness and at the same time would like to see a diplomatic detente in Eastern Asia. He also sees American-Japanese relations entering a period of tension and delicacy.

A short book by Zbigniew Brzezinski, *The Fragile Blossom: Crisis and Change in Japan* (New York: Harper and Row, 1972), likewise sees American-Japanese relations entering an era of uncertainty. He suggests that while on the surface Japan appears stable, there are problems and tensions which could erupt suddenly.

A new book by Donald C. Hellmann, *Japan and East Asia: The New International Order* (New York: Praeger, 1972), explores the expanded role Japan will likely assume in Asia and its implications for American-Japanese relations. Professor Hellmann, who teaches at the University of Washington, takes the view that Japan must develop nuclear arms if she is to participate actively in Asian politics. In *Arms, Yen and Power: The Japanese Dilemma* (New York: Dunellen, 1971), John Emmerson comes to a different conclusion. He believes that Japan will not seek to exert military power in Asia in the 1970s. He spent many years in Japan as an American diplomat, and has drawn on his long experience as well as on conversations with Asian leaders in writing his book.

Art and Literature

Since my field is politics, I do not feel competent to enter into an extended discussion of reading material in art and literature. I will, therefore, confine my remarks to a few items I have found helpful. Shuichi Kato's *Form, Style, Tradition: Reflections on Japanese Art and Society* (Berkeley: University of California Press, 1971) is an English translation by John Bester of a series of essays originally published in Japanese. Professor Kato, who now teaches at the Free University of Berlin, writes about art, artists, and creativity. He makes the interesting point that what we have in Japan today is not "Westernization" but, rather, "internationalization." He feels that Japanese artists, architects, and musicians are now beginning to express themselves in an international society using an international language.

A older book which is full of insightful comments on Japanese culture is *Meeting with Japan* by Fosco Maraini, an Italian scholar who lived in Japan for many years (New York: Viking Press, 1960). His account is discursive and personal.

Finally, I should say something about contemporary Japanese literature. Some of the best Japanese novels are being translated into English by a small group of gifted translators. I would suggest that readers start with Yasunari Kawabata's novels, *Snow Country* (New York: Alfred A. Knopf, 1956) and *Thousand Cranes* (New York: Alfred A. Knopf, 1958), both translated with great skill by Edward G. Seidensticker of the University of Michigan. The late Kawabata was awarded the Nobel Prize in Literature in 1968.

Some readers may find Japanese novels hard to understand as they often lack the sort of formal plot we are used to seeing in American fiction. However, they are rich in symbolism, depictions of emotional states, and psychological insights. Those who have the patience to develop a taste for Japanese novels will find them rewarding.

INDEX

Family, 27, 47
Farmers, 64
Farmers, support of Liberal
    Democratic party by, 63
Feudalism, 10-20, 21, 23, 30, 32
Foreign investments, 71, 72, 101
Foreign policy, 22, 25, 98-108
Foreign trade, 70-71, 88-89, 101
Forty-seven *ronin*, 49

Geographical features, 3
Government and business, 61
Gross National Product, 58, 62, 70,
    75
Groups, 29-46
Groups, structure of, 32-35
Guilds of specialized workers (*be*), 30

Hierarchy of social groups, 32, 41
Housing, 75-76, 78, 90

Ikeda, Hayato, 62, 94
Income-doubling plan, 62
"Independence of the Supreme Com-
    mand" of army and navy, 25
Individualism, 24, 27
Industrial organization, 35
Industrialization, beginnings of, 21
Industrialization in Asia, 89
Industries moving abroad, 85
Inflation, 56
Intellectuals and free thought, 24, 26
International trade, 15
International understanding, 108
Internationalism, 100-101
Investment in productive facilities, 67
Issun Boshi, 41-42
Ito, Prince Hirobumi, 22
Izanagi and Izanami, 1-2

Japanese gardens, 53
Japanese language, 6
Japanese society, 27
Japan's surrender in 1945, 26, 55

Kabuki theater, 15, 49
Kahn, Herman, 84, 107
Kamakura, government established
    in, 10
Karma, 5

Kato, Shuichi, 5
Kokutai, 24
Korea, 22, 106

Labor shortage, 36, 67, 84, 85
Labor unions, 40
Laborers, 35, 44, 51
Land, high cost of, 78
Legitimacy of parliamentary regime,
    96
Leisure, 87
Liberal Democratic party, 58, 60, 63,
    80, 104
Lifetime employment, 36
Lifton, Robert J., 50

Marxist ideology, 94
Mass communications, 25
Mass transit, 79-80
Meiji Emperor, 20, 23
Meiji period, 20-24
Meiji reforms, 21-22
Meiji Restoration, 20
Merchant class, 15
Ministry of International Trade and
    Industry, 61, 62, 86
Minobe, Tatsukichi, 25
Modernization during Meiji period,
    21-24
Money in politics, 60
Mythology, 1-3, 4, 5

Nakane, Chie, 32, 34
National defense, 20, 21, 22, 25, 57,
    101, 105, 106, 107
National defense spending, 58, 107
National isolation, 12-14, 20
Nationalism, 101, 103
Nature, Japanese attitudes towards,
    52
Nenko system of employment, 36
Neutrality, 101
Nixon, Richard, 104
"Nixon shock," 104
Nonverbal communication, 48
Nuclear arms, 106, 107
Nuclear attack, 106

Occupation of Japan, 26-27, 57, 98
Oda, Nobunaga, 10

ABOUT THE AUTHOR

Born in Seattle, Washington, Professor Nobutaka Ike attended public schools in that city and was graduated from the University of Washington in 1940. During World War II, he taught Japanese language at the U.S. Navy Language School in Boulder, Colorado. After he was awarded a doctorate in political science by The Johns Hopkins University in 1949, Professor Ike became Curator of the Japanese Collection of the Hoover Institution on War, Revolution, and Peace at Stanford University, serving in that post until 1957. In 1958, he joined the Department of Political Science at Stanford. He has received Ford Foundation and Rockefeller Foundation grants for study in Japan and has been a visiting professor at the University of California in Berkeley, the University of Michigan, the International Christian University of Tokyo, and, most recently, the University of the Philippines. Professor Ike is the editor of *Japan's Decision for War* (1967); coauthor (with Junichi Kyogoku) of *Urban-Rural Differences in Voting Behavior in Japan* (1959); and he is author of *Beginnings of Political Democracy in Japan* (1950), *Japanese Politics: An Introductory Survey* (1957), and *Japanese Politics: Patron-Client Democracy* (1972).